# Faithful Living

# Faithful Living:

*Discipleship, Creed and Ethics*

Michael J. Leyden

scm press

Published in 2019 by SCM Press
Editorial office
3rd Floor, Invicta House,
108–114 Golden Lane,
London EC1Y 0TG, UK
www.scmpress.co.uk

SCM Press is an imprint of Hymns Ancient & Modern Ltd
(a registered charity)

Hymns Ancient & Modern® is a registered trademark of Hymns Ancient
& Modern Ltd
13A Hellesdon Park Road, Norwich,
Norfolk NR6 5DR, UK

British Library Cataloguing in Publication data

A catalogue record for this book is available
from the British Library

978 0 334 05819 9

Printed and bound by
CPI Group ( UK ) Ltd

# Contents

For Anna, Eliana and Simeon
with my love and gratitude always xxx

# Preface

The early seeds of thought for this book were planted a decade ago in lecture rooms at both St John's College, Nottingham, and All Saints Centre for Mission and Ministry, Warrington, where I was visiting lecturer in Christian doctrine and ethics. Those seeds have been nurtured and grown over the past seven years into something much more substantial and, hopefully, edifying through teaching systematic theology, ethics and liturgical theology at St Mellitus College. During this time my aim has been to hold doctrine, biblical exegesis, ethics and worship together as mutual and complementary sub-disciplines within the wider task of Christian *dogmatics*. By dogmatic theology I do not mean some unwavering, hard-lined or arrogant approach to Christianity; rather, dogmatics is the ancient discipline of explaining the fulness of the Christian gospel by considering its rational, practical and spiritual components.

Put another way, dogmatic theology attends to the widest and deepest meaning of the gospel of Jesus Christ by viewing and interpreting it through a variety of specifically focused 'lenses'. These lenses often overlap with the sub-disciplines you are likely to find in a university Department of Theology: biblical studies, systematic theology, Church history, practical theology, pastoral theology, liturgical theology, ethics and the rest. But unlike such a department, the ultimate goal of dogmatics is not the separation of disciplines through increasing specialization and methodological detachment, but their integration. Such bringing together of disciplines which dogmatics entails results, at its best, in a holistic sharpening of focus on the singular object of Christian devotion: the triune God made known in the birth, life, death, resurrection and ascension of Jesus. Dogmatic theology is, therefore, necessarily interdisciplinary and by its very nature confessional: it flourishes only in the context of an existing faithful, worshipping community trying to make lived sense of its confession of faith.[1] Dogmatics is, therefore, the kind of theology that resources Christian discipleship.

The reason for the absolute unity-in-distinction which holds these lenses together is that the most basic concern of Christian theology, the gospel, is *a single event* narrated in the story of Jesus Christ – a story in the past, present and future tenses – in which the world is judged, condemned, reconciled and redeemed by God. And because Jesus the God-human is, according to the Church's confession in the Chalcedonian Definition (451), entirely one identity without confusion, separation, division or change, the Church is not permitted to allow its thinking about and proclamation of his gospel to become fragmented, twisted, warped or diluted. Doing so would be to bear false witness to God who is revealed supremely and finally in Christ. Dogmatics is, therefore, complicated. It is also necessary for a healthy Church: one that knows what it believes and therefore knows how to live.

That said, considering Christian ethics as part of the dogmatic task is, surprisingly, uncommon. There are some stand-out examples from the past century (Karl Barth, Dietrich Bonhoeffer, Helmut Thielicke), but on the whole ethics has been so regarded as a practical discipline that it has become increasingly distanced from what are perceived to be conceptual discussions in doctrine, or historico-sociologico-linguistic arguments in biblical studies, or peculiar debates about niche texts in liturgical studies. (And no doubt these sub-disciplines have become beset with arguments that are less than helpful to Christian ethicists.) Furthermore, the situation worsens when we remember that Christian ethical reasoning walks a fine line between the Church and the world (since so often our deliberations take place in tortuous dialogue with those whose worldview and underlying commitments are not our own) and so Christians must make efforts to articulate a common vision for human flourishing which is aligned with, or palatable to, or at least interesting to, those outside the Church if it wants to have an impact. For the sake of the common good it is a worthy approach, but it usually means emptying Christianity of its most radical doctrinal claims and undermining the dogmatic nature of ethics by separating our thinking about what to do from our formal thinking about who we are and what we believe. Christian ethicists cannot rely on undefined moral sentiments such as 'justice' or 'equality' without considering their theological and doctrinal meaning and therefore the peculiar voice that Christian faith brings to these issues; nor can they avoid exclusive religious commitments altogether to garner general support for an idea; nor can they become pseudo-biblicist or biblio-centric and miss the power of a theological framework for moral discourse which helps us to see who we are and how we are to live in the light of who God is rather than simple, hardline obedience to biblical imperatives. Of course, not all Christian ethics work this way.

Working, as I do, in the context of training women and men for ordained ministry, it seems to me that asking future Church leaders to consider with utmost seriousness what difference the Church's proclamation about God and the world might make to their lives and the lives of those to whom they minister is of fundamental importance both to Christian discipleship and the Church's mission. If ethics were regarded as part of dogmatics, then the ensuing task of equipping Christians to live in ways that are consistent with their doctrinal beliefs, and then to articulate clearly to a watching world why they live as they do, would also be to equip a generation to proclaim the gospel afresh.

One helpful oddity of the Anglican tradition is that we carry our doctrinal commitments in our liturgy rather than in a separate doctrinal basis or statement of faith. It means that our doctrine 'hits the ground running' in worship, and worship in turn shapes us by always seeking to lead us in a Godward direction – the God revealed in Jesus Christ and witnessed in Scripture and Creed. For me, therefore, writing as an Anglican priest, it is necessary that the interplay between doctrine and ethics is framed liturgically, since worship and liturgy is the place where clearest expression is given to substantive content of Christian faith, i.e. the place where Christian theological commitments are most obviously laid out and invite our response. As the ancients used to say: *lex orandi, lex credendi – we believe what we pray and we pray what we believe.*[2] One of the sub-tasks of this book is to extend that idea and explore *lex vivendi* as an additional and necessary aspect of this dynamic: *we believe what we pray, and we pray what we believe, and our beliefs and prayers inform how we live.* Worship is the place where disciples are formed intellectually, spiritually and practically as they endeavour to order their lives in response to the gospel.[3]

Perhaps surprisingly to some, given its breadth and variety, Anglicanism is orthodox and its liturgies take the Bible and creeds very seriously, which means that what emerges from a study such as this one is not a denominational ethic but a *Christian* ethic. To be doubly sure that this present book connects beyond the Anglican fold, I have chosen to attend to only one universally consistent aspect of liturgical worship: the Nicene Creed.[4] (A more fulsome treatment of the ethical and moral impact of liturgical worship is a topic for another book.) I explain more of this in Chapter 1, but suffice to say now that if doctrine is often overlooked in ethical deliberation it is even rarer to see liturgical material used to shape moral discourse. But the potential for discipleship and mission is considerable, since thousands of churches around the world make the Nicene Creed part of their weekly gathered worship. Identifying and exploring the ethical implications of liturgy is the underlying vision of this book, and this seems wholly consistent with the dogmatic task outlined above. Nowhere will I attempt to make the case that ethics should be thought of in this way, but rather I assume it from the beginning and work out the rest of the book on that basis by investigating the implications of our doctrinal commitments for our daily decisions and actions.

I am extremely grateful to all the students who have helped

me to shape the present work by engaging, challenging, affirming and refining the ideas first delivered in lectures and now in print – and for the good grace and humour with which they have participated in my classes. To work one's craft in such places and among such people is a gift to any teacher, and has been, for me at least, nothing less than a sign of God's grace.

Of course, the ideas have been refined considerably in conversation with good friends and outstanding colleagues. I am especially grateful to Nicholas Anderson, Helen and Pete Chantry, Simon Chesters, Claire Cooke, Simon Cuff, Ben and Alison Fulford, Lincoln Harvey, Joe Kennedy, Mark Knight, Donna Lazenby, Anna Leyden, Jonathan Phillips, Steve Torr, Carys Walsh and Jane Williams, whose comradeship and friendship has shaped the author and his work for the good. And to my parents and parents-in-law, Jan and Al, Brian and Mary, whose support has always been without limit. I'm especially grateful to Jill Duff, now Bishop of Lancaster and my predecessor as Director of St Mellitus College North West, who has encouraged this project since its inception. Without her boundless energy and roaring enthusiasm it is doubtful it would have seen the light of day.

Being a scholar-priest is one thing, and being a parish-priest is oftentimes another; being both things at once is something quite different.[5] I am very grateful to the former Bishop of Liverpool, The Rt Revd James Jones; the current Bishop of Chester, The Rt Revd Dr Peter Forster; the Bishop of Derby (formerly Suffragan Bishop of Stockport), The Rt Revd Libby Lane; and the President of St Mellitus College and fellow cricket fan, The Rt Revd Dr Graham Tomlin, all of whom in different ways have enabled me to fulfil a dual-role ministry in parish and in theological education. I am convinced this pattern, though sometimes tricky, enriches both the students and the parishes in which I have served, as well as my own life. Over the years the people of St Barnabas Inham Nook, St Ann Rainhill, All Saints Weston with St Mark Shavington, and more recently St Peter at the Cross Chester, have taught me a great deal about the love of God, about grace and forgiveness, and about the importance of Church community for our mutual flourishing in Christ. They have also persevered through my sermons with good humour, including a series on the Nicene Creed, and offered helpful feedback on some of the key elements of this book. I am grateful to all of them, but most especially to the office holders at Weston and Shavington – the Church Wardens, Roger Bracey and Robert Galloway, and Licensed Lay Ministers (Readers), Margaret Hodgkinson, Ginny Lewis, Anna Leyden, and trainees Gaynor Bracey and Chris Neufeld – whose ministries are value-added in that place and brought richness to the community while allowing their then vicar time to think and write.

I must also thank David Shervington, commissioning editor at SCM Press, for his patient support and encouragement to get this project finished in the midst of a busy work-life, some family worries, and an ever-expanding 'to do' list. I am very grateful to him, and to God for him.

The final word of thanks must go to another, much smaller community: three people without whom my life would be considerably impoverished and this book would still be a thing of the imagination. To my wife, Anna, and our children, Eliana and Simeon, whose love and encouragement is much more than I deserve and whose sense of fun and enjoyment of family life has kept me grounded in what really matters to God, I express my deepest and unending thanks. To these three this book is dedicated.

### Notes

1 A critical account of the development of theology in a university context, and the challenge it provokes for Christians, can be found in John Webster, *Theological Theology: An Inaugural Lecture delivered before the University of Oxford on 28th October 1997* (Oxford: Clarendon Press, 1998).

2 Karl Barth described the phrase *lex orandi lex credendi* as 'one of the most profound descriptions of the theological method' in his

essay 'The Gift of Freedom' in his *The Humanity of God* (Louisville: Westminster John Knox, 1960), 90.

3 The Reformed theologian James K. A. Smith has been helpfully addressing these issues in his multi-volume *Cultural Liturgies* series. See, for example, the first volume, *Desiring the Kingdom: Worship, Worldview, and Cultural Formation* (Grand Rapids: Baker Academic, 2009), or the recent popular version, *You Are What You Love: The Spiritual Power of Habit* (Grand Rapids: Brazos, 2016).

4 See G. W. Bromiley's summary of the universal ecumenical impact of the Nicene Creed in the essay, 'Unity and Confession', in his *The Unity and Disunity of the Church* (Grand Rapids: Eerdmans, 1958), 75–82.

5 A really helpful account of this kind of dual ministry has recently been offered by Gerald Heistand and Todd Wilson, *The Pastor Theologian: Resurrecting an Ancient Vision* (Grand Rapids: Zondervan, 2015).

## The Nicene Creed

We believe in one God,
the Father, the Almighty,
maker of heaven and earth,
of all that is, seen and unseen.

We believe in one Lord, Jesus Christ, the only Son of God,
eternally begotten of the Father,
God from God, Light from Light,
true God from true God,
begotten, not made,
of one Being with the Father;
through him all things were made.
For us and for our salvation he came down from heaven,
was incarnate from the Holy Spirit and the Virgin Mary and
was made man.
For our sake he was crucified under Pontius Pilate;
he suffered death and was buried.
On the third day he rose again
in accordance with the Scriptures;
he ascended into heaven
and is seated at the right hand of the Father.
He will come again in glory to judge the living and the dead,
and his kingdom will have no end.

We believe in the Holy Spirit,
the Lord, the giver of life,
who proceeds from the Father and the Son,
who with the Father and the Son is worshipped and glorified,
who has spoken through the prophets.
We believe in one holy catholic and apostolic Church.
We acknowledge one baptism for the forgiveness of sins.
We look for the resurrection of the dead,
and the life of the world to come.

# 1

# Ethics by Implication

## Introduction

How should Christians live, and what differences might our faith make to the daily round of decisions and actions that make up our lives? These are questions you might hear on the lips of parishioners, thoughtful members of a youth group, enquiring ordinands and students of religion. But the fact that such questions need to be asked betrays a modern phenomenon in which the theological substance of faith – its basic claims about God, the world and everything else – has become separated from the stuff of everyday life, privatized and relegated to Sunday morning devotions and personal spirituality. Knowing how faith and actions relate to one another is no longer obvious. Nor is it much talked about. In a globalized context, theories of tolerance have dealt with religious claims by relativizing them.[1] And many Christians have colluded with it, though for different reasons. When Pope Francis criticized the US Presidential hopeful Donald Trump for the shallowness of his Christian faith in the light of revelations about his treatment of women and lies about political collusion, the Pontiff received criticism from other prominent Christians, including Trump's opponents Jeb Bush and Marco Rubio. Bush's interiorization of faith was explicit, and he would not be drawn on the Christian *quality* of Trump's behaviour: 'I honestly believe that's a relationship you have with your creator.'[2] Though the effort to not judge or offend means there may be widespread sympathy for such a sentiment, it masks a deeper (and overriding) commitment to individualism and consumerism. In such a cultural paradigm, faith is not only a personal matter (which it is) but a private matter (which it cannot be). To allow Trump's inconsistency without question sets a precedent in which what someone claims to believe and how they live need not integrate. Faith gets privatized, and privatized religion separates the intellectual content of faith, i.e. what we believe, from the practical content of faith, i.e. how we live, leading to the kind of anaemic faith that prevents congregations from understanding the practical value of theological commitments.

The questions with which I began this chapter reject this separation in favour of an integrated and holistic account of the Christian life. Integration means treating several distinct parts of something as a whole by linking each part within a wider framework of meaning. An integrated life avoids the fragmentation of human existence into individual moments, beliefs, habits or practices and instead pursues co-inherence as it highest good, choosing to treat the different parts – family, work, hobbies, religion, values, education, culture, sex and gender, and their related decisions and actions – as constituent ingredients of a single identity. What I do, where I am from, what I value, who I love, and what I believe are, among other things, all parts of who I am, or, perhaps more honestly, who I am becoming. A fragmented sense of self is not healthy. It manifests an inward denial of God's creative intention.

But, integration of parts does not necessarily mean equality of parts. We are not seeking to hold competing aspects in balance. For Christians, the 'religious' aspect of life necessarily impacts the whole sense of being and acting, because faith in the triune God has a determinative quality which stems from the worship of Christ as Lord. Such commitment is all encompassing, loving God with the heart, soul, mind and strength (Mark 12.30; Matt. 22.37; Luke 10.27). With this in mind, we might imagine a Christian aspiring to work as a school teacher or nurse or scientist, but it's tougher to believe she or he would aspire to dealing illegal narcotics or being a hired assassin since that work does not align with the teachings of Jesus: such jobs are innately destructive and opposed to the abundant life that Christ came to bring (John 10.10). The *challenge* of an integrated Christian life is in recognizing that it's not a given, but something we must learn to do as we learn to live in the light of the gospel. It is what we might otherwise call the challenge of *discipleship*. 'Discipleship ... is a matter of being taught to live ... it is about being accountable to Jesus ...'[3] The challenge is entailed in Jesus' call to the first disciples, 'come and follow me'. To follow somebody is not simply to trail behind them and journalistically document their lifestyle choices, or provide an audience for their activities. Following in the Christian sense involves learning from, and growing with, and integrating into, the life of faith that is centred on Jesus Christ to the exclusion of all others. To meet the challenge of discipleship appropriate discernment is needed.

In what follows I reject the notion of separating theology from everyday life by suggesting an approach to discipleship that integrates belief and practice in their more formal guises as doctrine and ethics. It might seem strange to suggest that these two aspects of the faith should need integrating at all, but for many the central beliefs of the Church can feel remote and removed from the concerns of everyday life. One of the tasks of pastoral ministry is to help people connect their relationship with Jesus Christ and their place in his Church with their everyday experiences, decisions and actions. At no point in this book will I try to establish whether Christian beliefs ought to make a difference to the lives Christians lead. Even the most ardent atheist assumes that they will (and can be quick to identify our hypocrisy when they don't). Rather, I take a more explicatory approach to the topic by presuming that the material and theological substance of Christianity is intellectually, emotionally and spiritually formative, and ought also, therefore, to be ethically formative. Following this instinct means that further resources for discipleship become available.

Such thinking has long been a part of the Christian tradition.

Take, for example, that great preacher, Augustine of Hippo, who saw theology as the peculiar and distinguishing foundation of an integrated life: 'I am speaking now to Christians; if you believe otherwise, hope otherwise, and love otherwise, then you must also live otherwise.'[4] The sermon was delivered sometime in the early fifth century,[5] somewhere in North Africa (most likely in Augustine's episcopal city of Hippo Regius, in modern day Algeria) to a gathering of disciples. It is clear from the message that the bishop trusted the congregation really did *believe* the right things about God, the world and themselves, but he also feared that in the face of the temptations of the orgiastic celebration offered by the New Year feast they would not *live* as though those beliefs should make a difference. Perhaps they would forget, or maybe they were ill-equipped to 'join the dots' between beliefs and actions. On the basis of a short exposition of Christ's saving work, Augustine called the congregation to aspire to St Paul's exhortation to 'walk as children of light' (Eph. 5.7–8), and thus reject the behaviours associated with pagan ritual, drunkenness and lasciviousness. If they were to think through the Apostle's question, 'what accord can there be between the Lord's temple and idols?' (2 Cor. 6.14–16), they would see the answer is none at all, since the God of Jesus Christ has no equal and thus cannot be compared with the false gods of the idols. These Christians were to 'believe in him who is the one and only true God' and then show that belief, Augustine argued, in concrete decisions that 'demonstrate faith by … action'.[6] Religious belief alone, as if fragmented and detached from other parts of life, is not good enough; the Algerian disciples were called to an integrated life (cf. Jas 2.18–24).

Of course, if we stop to think about it, ethical deliberation works just like that for most people, either implicitly or explicitly. We see it when a person acts contrary to their professed beliefs and we are moved to question their honesty and integrity. Our culture expects transparency in order to connect someone's actions to their motivating commitments, no matter how peculiar or (un)religious their worldview.[7] That said, it is not always easy to make connections and the reality of integration may be complex. To take a prime example, Christian doctrines – which we might think of as the codified form of Christian belief – can feel dry, conceptual and irrelevant because they're intellectually demanding and sometimes impractical. (Think of the kinds of questions with which we started and the parishioners who might be asking them.) The religious jargon that often accompanies them, as well as the years of debate and argument, means that doctrines seems at some distance from the practicalities of ethics and morality. It's not that Christians don't really believe them, as the scene from Hippo Regius reminds us, but that doctrines are not obviously useful in everyday life circumstances.

The twentieth-century theologian Otto Weber pointed out that the historic separation of doctrine and ethics within the Church was not due to poor pastoral ministry or bad bishops, but stemmed from changes wrought at the Enlightenment, during which time often difficult and complicated Christian beliefs failed to be integrated into the prevailing rationalist worldview. This, he argued, led the Church to adopt a specifically *'non-theological ...* conception of the "Christian Life" which was independently examinable, describable, and explainable'.[8] Why wouldn't that happen in such a context? After all, Christian beliefs *are* inherently irrational and weird. Consider the improbable claim to uniqueness associated with the resurrection of Jesus, or the mathematical challenge of the doctrine of the Trinity. In the face of such absurdities, other (related but not identical) ideas like love, forgiveness and equality are much more sensible and acceptable. However, Weber's cautionary response to this gives us pause for thought: he argued that what gives meaning to the adjective 'Christian' as it is applied to doctrine is the same when applied to 'ethics': namely, belief that the triune God is at work in the world through Jesus Christ and the Holy Spirit, and this is witnessed in Scripture and summed up in the Church's ecumenical creeds. In other words, Christians cannot easily abandon the Church's historic doctrines because they are a matter of identity; Christians are those who believe *these* things (or at least are somehow related to those who believe these things). So, Weber wrote, 'to make ethics autonomous ... would imply that there are special criteria available for ethics. But we cannot find such criteria'.[9] Any ethic that desires to be Christian must be rooted in Christianity's theological substance of which doctrines are the codified theological form: separation and fragmentation is not possible, and ultimately not helpful for the challenges of discipleship.

Thus my concern in this book is for what I think of as an *integrated ethics of discipleship* which might position itself as an answer to the question: *what kinds of lifestyle choices, decisions and actions might be implied for contemporary disciples by the theological substance of the Christian faith?*[10] As will become clear, I think what is required is a particular approach to Christian moral reasoning that prioritizes practical catecheses and can thus resource Christian discipleship in the local church. It does so by attending to the ethical meaning of doctrinal statements.

## Towards a Doctrinally Motivated Ethics

Probably the most common approach to Christian ethics found in introductory textbooks or primers begins with an immediate quandary, problem or 'hard case',[11] and then help is sought from a recognized canon of theological resources (Scripture, tradition, reason, experience). We might think, for example, of what to do about an unwanted pregnancy. Ethicists here use the resources to assess and evaluate which of a range of possible responses (abortion included) is most appropriate. It might involve deliberation on the sanctity of life in biblical theology, or feminist theology's recovery of female agency, or ecumenical discussion of the meaning of personhood, or all three. The quandary itself is the impetus for moral reasoning and guides which resources are used. If done well the discussion neatly provides a concrete answer to a concrete question, after which a precedent may be set that can, in turn, shape wider discourse on other related topics.

While the ethics of hard cases is common, it is not easily marshalled to answer our question here, where the presenting problem is not a specific quandary but the more general puzzle of how to live with Christian theological beliefs. Another approach is needed. Michael Banner helps us to see this when he counsels ethical discourse against 'becoming so besotted with hard cases as to take the view, in effect, that they comprise the scope of its tasks and responsibilities'.[12] Common sense tells us he is correct. Ethics has a more wide-ranging responsibility because life involves more than lolloping from quandary to quandary. What is needed is something bigger: a mode of ethical reasoning that captures and locates our momentary problems within a fuller description of human existence, mapping-out the kind of life Christians might lead when they're *not* trying to navigate the difficult issues as well as when they are. This means ethical discourse, which is descriptive, explicating human existence in direct relation to the theological substance of the Christian faith. For this, I suggest, it is necessary to reverse the trend found in some textbooks to treat doctrines as secondary resources called to serve the solution to a particular moral quandary and instead to prioritize attentiveness to doctrines as identity-conferring commitments which orientate an integrated Christian life.

Doctrines are the Church's most deeply held beliefs. They are the products of lengthy reflection on Christian experiences of encounter with God in Jesus Christ, and the subsequent effort to make sense of the nature and identity of this God and ourselves as his creatures. They grow out of careful engagement with Scripture as the divinely appointed witness to God's work (2 Tim. 3.15–17).[13] Scripture's authority does not consist in the powers of its human authors or interpreters but, as John Webster has argued, because 'Holy Scripture is the result of divine movement; it is generated not simply by human spontaneity but by the moving power of the Holy Spirit', and therefore it has a 'Spirit-bestowed capacity to quicken theology to truthful thought and speech.'[14] Scripture is in one sense a human product that results from encounter with God, but in another it is *inspired* writing. This means that it holds a status more than personal or corporate memoir because of the presence of another vitalizing power – the Spirit. The Church's doctrines are a construct of the community as it has made sense of its subsequent encounters with God in the light of Scripture.[15] Doctrines attempt to summarize and display the gospel by fixing points of reference for our talk about God that are faithful to Scripture and therefore to Jesus Christ. Doctrines are, therefore, derivatively authoritative in proportion to their faithfulness to Scripture's witness. Doctrines do not replace Scripture because they are contingent upon it, but they do act as shorthand systematic summaries of its content as it has been understood and appropriated by the Church under the tutelage of the Holy Spirit. The corporate nature of doctrines – that they articulate the *Church's* faith – means they are also the benchmark by which Christians in every generation measure their speech about God, looking back to what has gone before to make sense of what is happening now because the triune God is consistently God's self in all encounters with human beings.[16]

In ethical discourse, doctrines help us to delineate appropriately the space for human action by showing what human existence (which includes human action) is in relation to God. Theologians call this *moral ontology*. It means that doctrines function like both the pitch and the boundary rope in a cricket match, scoping the centre and the limits of what is most important before any consideration of how to do ethics can occur in the outfield. Doctrines, as identity-conferring commitments, are, therefore, orientational. They remind us that God is Creator and we are creatures, and this kind of claim has significant ethical impact. As we describe who God is and what God does we also step closer to describing our own meaning, purpose and direction as bound up with him through

Christ and purposed for the good works that he determines (Eph. 2.10). Again, this is not a static notion of divine-human relations, but is rooted in the biblical idea of encounter.

Theologically speaking, the principal defining encounter with God happened on the first Easter Sunday at the entrance to an empty tomb when some disciples met with the living Jesus Christ. There, Jesus was revealed to be more than another prophet, teacher, healer, sage or revolutionary, and was declared to be the Son of God in power by the resurrection (Rom. 1.4). With it came the impetus for theological reflection and the early stages of the gestation of trinitarian theology as the God of the Old Testament was (eventually) understood to be more than previously thought. Indeed, much of the New Testament is given over to making sense of who this God is and what the good news about Christ means for us creatures (as any cursive reading of the Pauline epistles can demonstrate).[17] Viewed thus, the horizon of ethics is the God whose creative and redemptive purpose we fulfil with our whole lives as adopted children and heirs with Christ (Rom. 8.14–17). It is a question of identity and how doctrines, if taken seriously, commit Christians to do ethics *as* Christians. For example, if God is Creator, then we are creatures; if God is Love, then we are the objects of divine affection; if God is reconciler, then we are forgiven sinners; if God is life, then we are those about whom death does not have the final word; if God is redeemer, then we are those hoping for and anticipating the renewal of creation. Doctrines are thus to be regarded as identity-conferring commitments: believing them radically implicates Christian disciples in their entirety, i.e. the whole of each Christian life is brought into the direct purview of God (cf. 1 Pet. 2.9). Ethical deliberation means moving from these commitments towards the kinds of decisions and actions that they imply.

The point is helpfully illustrated in St Paul's deft move towards ethics in the first five verses of Romans chapter 12, following a lengthy theological treatise on sin, salvation in Jesus Christ, baptism, grace, the Church, God's promises, and Israel in chapters 1–11. It is introduced with the adverb 'therefore', *oὖv*, indicating that Paul structures his commands to live sacrificially, to be transformed intellectually, to think with humility and appropriate sobriety, and to seek the wellbeing of the whole community as the logical corollary of the Christ-centred work of salvation he had just described. As Charles Cranfield has helpfully said, 'the implication of this "therefore" is that Christian ethics are theologically motivated … the *oὖv* makes clear right from the start the theocentric nature of all truly Christian moral effort; for it indicates that the source from which such effort springs is … the saving deed of God itself'.[18] This 'saving deed' is the material substance of Christianity and the *sine qua non* of Christian ethics, the work of Jesus Christ. In structuring the relationship between doctrine and ethics in this way, St Paul configured the ethical task as a (whole-life) response to God's grace. What we might ordinarily call discipleship. In the usual cultic practices of the Old Testament the sacrifices died on the altar. This was their end-goal and meaning. Christians, however, are sacrifices that live in the perpetual state of offering themselves wholly to God. For ones such as these, doctrinal theology does not become relevant only when we face an ethical dilemma. Rather, doctrines describe and articulate (and thus confer) aspects of the bigger reality in which our lives make sense and within which, therefore, all of our decisions and actions must co-inhere. In other words, as Weber suggested, rootedness in Christian doctrine is necessary if ethics is to be *Christian* ethics because doctrines help us to articulate and understand who we are as disciples of Jesus Christ. It is doubly necessary if the question *what kinds of lifestyle choices, decisions and actions might be implied for contemporary disciples by the theological substance of the Christian faith?* is to have any hope of an answer. My approach is to frame the ethics of an integrated life as the discernment of the practical implications of Christian doctrinal commitments.

## Ethics by Implication

I am aware that proposing to reason from doctrines towards
ethics might suggest that there are fewer obvious rules to be
obeyed, thereby seeming to remove ethics from the traditional
nexus of right and wrong. The result is that ethical deliberation
can feel at once more spacious and more confused. The
spaciousness comes from the freedom to explore and consider
all options, weighing and testing them against the identity-
conferring commitments that doctrines entail. It opens up the
world of moral reasoning to a range of possibilities and it can
be liberating to think of our lives as blank canvases in which we
make decisions for no other reason than to reflect our identity
as recipients of the gospel of grace. But the confusion comes
when we realize that between the pitch and the boundary, the
outfield can be an unpredictable and disordered place. Knowing
the terrain and knowing how to navigate it really does matter if
we are to stay on our feet. So it is with ethics. Without a means
of navigating the space, ethics can feel unwieldy and unfocused
and that is usually, in the end, less than helpful as decision-
making is nearly impossible. The dilemma has not escaped me.
Though I take criticism of the quandary approach seriously, I
do not want to make the equal and opposite mistake of acting
as if specificity does not matter in favour of vague, obscure
or idealized descriptions of what contemporary Christian
discipleship might be.

My solution is rooted in the reversal of the usual role of
doctrine from resourcing an ethical quandary to orientating
an integrated Christian ethics of discipleship, denoted in the
question, *what kinds of lifestyle choices, decisions and actions
might be implied for contemporary disciples by the theological
substance of the Christian faith?* The word *implication* has
its roots in the Latin for 'entanglement' or 'integration'. In
philosophical terms, *implication* is a kind of logical inference
in which consequences or conclusions (which are referenced
with the letter '*q*') may be drawn from a proposition or set

of propositions (which are referenced with the letter '$p$'). It has been borrowed by theologians such as Paul Lehman as a shorthand to explain how it is that some 'theological statements have ethical meaning'.[19] Though Lehman recognizes it is not true of all such statements, where it is, the strength of the inference rests on the formal logic that governs the relationship between $p$ and $q$. The more necessary the implication, the stricter the logic and the more resolutely we need to hold to the compound relationship ($p \rightarrow q$) in whatever circumstance. My preference is for an intuitive rather than strict construction: I am not arguing that the doctrinal propositions I discuss ($p$) will of necessity always lead to the particular set of ethical consequences I suggest ($q$), but I am experimenting with what may be logically implied if we allow the Church's identity-conferring doctrinal commitments to orientate us first, and then act in ways that are consistent with those commitments. Or, to put it another way, I am interested in what imperatives may be derived or inferred from theological indicatives.

My goal throughout is to be intentional and particular about Christian doctrines, but also more open-ended about the implications and ethical applications that follow (to that extent it is less helpful to think of the ethical discussions as imperatival). I want this book to stimulate thoughtfulness among regular worshippers about both doctrine and ethics. That is to say that since I am not driven by finding a solution to a presenting problem my approach is more relaxed and, I hope, inviting. It is to think through what an integrated ethics of discipleship might mean in its fullest terms. As Philip Ziegler has put it, 'when we make discipleship our theme we ask the following question: how ought we to characterize a human life which, having been justified, redeemed and reconciled to God *by* Jesus Christ, is now given time and place in which to live anew *in* and *with* Christ?'[20] Ethics of this kind is indicative rather than prescriptive, deducing which actions are best by way of implication not imposition, and rooting the discussion in our identity as Christ's people. Again, Ziegler helpfully clarifies the point, 'the disciple is not in pursuit of an ideal, not even an embodied ideal. She is rather labouring in the Spirit to remain in the wake of Jesus's own singular work ... with an eye on the difference that the dawning of the reign of God makes.'[21] The point is to work from the disciple's position as recipient of Christ's saving work and anticipant of the coming Kingdom *towards* actions that are consistent with that identity and contribute to the Kingdom's coming. We do this precisely by inferring concrete behaviours from prior theological commitments and thus drawing the kind of direct line between belief and practice that Augustine's Hippo Regius sermon invited. Undoubtedly, much more could be said about each of the doctrines I discuss in this book. My goal is not an exhaustive composition, but is to give an indication of what is possible for Christian moral reasoning of this type, especially in the context of a local church or theological college (which have been my primary contexts for working on this material). Before proceeding to an overview of the chapters that follow, I want to add a word about my choice to focus on the Nicene Creed as a doctrinal text.

## The Nicene Creed

So far, I have advocated a theological ethics that begins with identity-conferring doctrinal commitments, but some would argue that I am about to fail spectacularly by shaping this book around the Nicene Creed. Creeds are confessions of faith and affirmations made by baptismal candidates, ordinands and gathered congregations that show they really are part of the historic Christian community and that they will uphold the Church's witness to God in the present and the future. Creeds are often short, containing only the minimal necessary theological substance. Their proper home is the liturgical order of service (often compulsory in baptismal services, ordinations and the Eucharist) which guides and structures the worship of God's people. Doctrinal discussion and debate is something else. It is often much lengthier, and more detailed. It can also be more partisan and antagonistic. Indeed, the history of many thousands of denominations worldwide is little more than a history of doctrinal disagreement. Creeds are summary confessions, where doctrinal treatises are often partisan explanations. But it is precisely for its ecumenical and confessional nature that I think the Nicene Creed is a helpful platform on which to build an integrated ethics of discipleship. Confession is, I suggest, a specific form of doctrinal theology: proclamation. Consider this definition by John Webster,

> Before it is proposition or oath of allegiance, the confession of the church is a cry of acknowledgement of the unstoppable miracle of God's mercy. Confession, we might say by way of definition, is that event in which the speech of the church is arrested, grasped, and transfigured by the self-giving presence of God. To confess is to cry out in acknowledgement of the sheer gratuity of what the gospel declares, that in and as the man Jesus, in the power of the Holy Spirit, God's glory is the glory of his self-giving, his radiant generosity. Very simply, to confess is to indicate the glory of Christ (2 Corinthians 8:23).[22]

Confessions are created in *response* to God's activity; acknowledging and receiving the goodness of God's mercy and enjoying the status of adoption and belonging that that mercy makes real for us. They are forms of praise and worship, in which creatures rehearse and affirm the story of God's acts alongside and for their fellow creatures as works of witness. They are thus the means by which Christians 'make that story and that affirmation their own'.[23] Credal confessions are formalized and codified doctrinal statements, in which the Church's understanding of the gospel is laid bare. And like doctrines, confessions are identity conferring as markers of our allegiance to the God who is known in the gospel of Jesus

Christ and no other. We see this at baptisms and ordinations, where the corporate body of the Church confesses the credal faith as an act of worship and a statement of identity because the candidates will subsequently take up a new place within the life of the Church. We see it too in Holy Communion where, in the Anglican tradition at least, the public confession of the faith of Nicaea is the culmination of the Service of the Word as the summary of Scripture's witness before leading into the Liturgy of the Sacrament.

The Nicene Creed has other things going for it in this regard. It is an ecumenical confession, forged in the midst of debate between hundreds of bishops and theologians over a period of several months, and is offered as the answer to a conundrum about the nature of the gospel of Christ. And it is still in use across the world today in most of the major Christian traditions as a common point of unity and consistency across contexts and cultures. The Nicene Creed is a gospel confession, witnessing to the triune work of God the Creator, Reconciler and Redeemer. To confess it is to frame the meaning, purpose and direction of creation in the light of the Christ-event, past, present and future. To confess the creed as a disciple is to be so confident in this God as to orientate our lives toward Christ, declaring allegiance there and nowhere else. The Nicene Creed is, therefore, doctrinal, articulating the Church's understanding of its encounters with God in the light of the scriptural witness and thus being useful for helping Christians know what is true[24] and giving shape to the Church's ministry as a normative 'grammar for Christian preaching and teaching'.[25] This is doubly so since most church historians agree that, where the Apostles' Creed was always to be said by those being baptized and their godparents, the Nicene Creed was always intended for bishops and priests, i.e. those exercising pastoral and theological leadership within the Church. It explicitly states that its claims are 'according to the Scriptures' and thus requires us to think about the Creed as Scriptural summary, and *vice versa* to follow biblical interpretation that is consistent with the Creed 'for the two are seen as correlative and interdependent'.[26] In this way, the Nicene Creed has a defining role in Christianity: it tells us what Christians believe. As we learn this, we can think also about how we should live in response to it. As such the Nicene Creed does some of the significant theological work I was describing in the last section: it orientates disciples by teaching core doctrines that are identity conferring, and fixing both the theological centre and boundary of what is legitimately Christian. It is, therefore, my starting point for an integrated ethics of discipleship.

## Outlining the Book

As has, no doubt, just become clear, this book will annoy some readers for sidestepping the complexities of historical context, political machinations, socio-cultural dynamics, and the development of doctrine which are bound up with the story of the Nicene Creed. Perhaps I should be sorry, but I am not – and for that I ask readers' patience and absolution. While such considerations probably do matter in other areas, I will mention them only where it helps to bring theological clarity in order to say what matters ethically. My only agenda in doing so is to keep the first intention of this book in view, namely to sketch one account of Christian ethics that grows out of identity-conferring doctrinal commitments rooted in the regular liturgical practice of credal confession.

Each chapter considers a clause of the Nicene Creed, discussing both its theological and moral meaning. To that extent the chapters may be regarded more or less standalone (though the book as a whole is trying to make a singular point about resourcing discipleship). The first part of each chapter outlines theological considerations within the broader biblical and doctrinal structures of Christian orthodoxy; the second part considers an ethical implication that may be inferred from that discussion for the choices, decisions and actions facing a contemporary disciple. In each chapter the symbol ***** marks the separation of part one from part two. I do not pretend that these chapters are exhaustive, nor that I am offering the final word on any matter. Indeed, some of the issues discussed were not and could not ever have been in the minds of the bishops and advisors at Nicaea. My only apology for this is to say my first concern is for the Creed's potential for ethics and discipleship today. I regard the approach as somewhat experimental: liturgy and the Creeds are not often cited in ethical deliberation. But it does seem to me a necessary and legitimate task to think about contemporary life in the light of the gospel and many of us encounter the Church's ancient understanding of that in credal and liturgical texts. To help the reader think with and beyond the proposals I am making, each chapter ends with some suggestions for reading and a few brief questions to stimulate further thinking.

The five chapters that follow this one focus on particular concrete actions in relation to wider ethical themes. Chapter 2, 'We Believe in God: Community and Morality', considers the task of corporate deliberation and what might be necessary to enable constructive conciliarity. Chapter 3, 'Maker of Heaven and Earth: Consuming Our Fellow Creatures', attends to the doctrine of creation, and what is implied for our consumption of non-human animals if we take seriously the two-pronged belief that the world is not ours to do with as we wish and that God has gifted to all its parts meaning and purpose. Chapter 4, 'In One Lord, Jesus Christ: Political Participation', attends to the political nature of the claim that Jesus Christ is Lord and what this implies for Christians within Western democracy. Chapter 5, 'Conceived of the Holy Spirit, Born of the Virgin Mary: Disability and Humanity', considers contemporary attitudes towards disability and human flourishing in the light of the humanity of Christ. Chapter 6, 'Suffered Death and was Buried …': Suffering' reviews contemporary arguments about quality of life in the light of the suffering of Jesus Christ and questions the idea that dignity must mean a life free from suffering.

The next two chapters discuss the character of Christian moral reasoning, rather than the concrete instances in which ethical decisions should be made. Chapter 7, 'On the Third Day He Rose Again: Hope and Moral Vision' argues that the principal posture of Christian ethical discourse is hopefulness because the Christian life is enacted in the metaphysical space between resurrection and parousia. Chapter 8, 'The Lord and Giver of Life: The Holy Spirit and the Christian Life', locates the discipline of Christian ethics formally within a worshipping community by considering the place of prayer in Christian moral reasoning and the life of discipleship.

The book concludes with a proposal or proto-manifesto for church leaders with Chapter 9, 'Communion of Saints, and Forgiveness of Sin': The Church and Practical Catechesis'. It suggests both the need for and the possibility of adult catechesis for contemporary discipleship. This is not as straightforward as a preaching series on the creed, but requires a serious reckoning with the way we think about our identity-conferring commitments holistically, so that Christian doctrines are accessible and understandable both intellectually and practically. Put another way, it requires us to be leaders who enable afresh that ancient vision for the ordinary Christian life which I discussed in the preface: *lex credendi, lex orandi, lex vivendi* – worship, theology and practice robustly intertwined. The suggestions made in the final chapter are not exhaustive, and I am not the best pastor. Indeed, others can add to and correct it. But I end there because I think it is the first implication of a book of this kind, and I hope it helps.

### Notes

1 For a critical view of this development see Donald Carson, *The Gagging of God: Christianity Confronts Pluralism* (Leicester: Apollos, 1996). More critically engaged accounts can be found in Gavin D'Costa, *Theology in the Public Square: Church, Academy, and Nation* (Oxford: Blackwell, 2005); and Stephen Holmes (ed.), *Public Theology in Cultural Engagement* (Milton Keynes: Paternoster, 2008). A helpful collection with particular focus on post-modernism is Philip Sampson, Vinay Samuel and Chris Sugden (eds), *Faith and Modernity* (Oxford: Regnum Books, 1997).

2 Norman Wirzba, 'Is Christian Faith a Private Matter', *HuffPost*,

February 21 2017, www.huffpost.com/entry/is-christian-faith-a-priv_b_9284910 (accessed November 2018).

3 Wirzba, 'Is Christian Faith A Private Matter?'

4 Augustine, 'Sermon 198: On January 1, Against the Pagans', in his *Sermons 184–229Z: On the Liturgical Seasons,* trans. Edmund Hill (New York: New City Press, 1993), 70.

5 There is some dispute about the year, with some arguing that it was preached around 404 AD and others that it was 420 AD. See Michele Renee Salzman, 'Christian Sermons against Pagans: The Evidence from Augustine's Sermons on the New Year and on the Sack of Rome in 410', in *The Cambridge Companion to Attila the Hun,* ed. Michael Maas (Cambridge: Cambridge University Press, 2014), 347; and Edmund Hill's brief commentary in Augustine, Sermon 198, 70.

6 Augustine, Sermon 198, 68.

7 Though, only 30 years ago Liberal Christian scholarship was less convinced by particularity in ethical reason, and argued for a universal human ethic. See Alister McGrath, 'Doctrine and Ethics', in *Journal of the Evangelical Theological Society* Vol. 34.2 (1991), 145–56.

8 Otto Weber, *Foundations of Dogmatics: Volume 1* (Grand Rapids: Eerdmans, 1981), 63.

9 Weber, *Foundations,* 68.

10 This is an adaptation and expansion of a question Paul Lehman asked in his, *Ethics in a Christian Context* (Westport, CT: Greenwood Press, 1963), 26.

11 Michael Banner labels this whole approach 'the ethics of hard cases'. See his *The Ethics of Everyday Life: Moral Theology, Social Anthropology, and the Imagination of the Human* (Oxford: Oxford University Press, 2016), 8–13.

12 Banner, *Ethics of Everyday Life,* 9.

13 For a very helpful discussion of the the role of Scripture in the life of the Church, see Carl E. Braaten and Robert Jenson (eds.), *Reclaiming the Bible for the Church* (Edinburgh: T&T Clark, 1995). And on the topic of the Bible as Holy Scripture, see John Webster, *Holy Scripture: A Dogmatic Sketch* (Cambridge: Cambridge University Press, 2003).

14 John Webster, *Holiness* (London: SCM Press, 2003), 18–19.

15 For more on the complexity of this relationship between Scripture and Creed see Scott Swain, 'A Ruled Reading Reformed: The Role of the Church's Confession in Biblical Interpretation', *International Journal of Systematic Theology* Vol. 14.2 (2012), 177–93.

16 Karl Barth has argued that making sense of the statement 'God is' is the central and most potent task of Christian theology. See his

*Church Dogmatics II/1: The Doctrine of God* (Edinburgh: T&T Clark, 1957), 257.

17 Robert Jenson helpfully notes that throughout scripture the effort to answer the question 'who is God?' is always conducted by denoting God's works. The God of the Bible is the One who does the things we read about in the Bible. See his *The Triune Identity: God According to the Gospel* (Eugene, OR: Wipf and Stock, 1982/2002).

18 C. E. B. Cranfield, *A Critical and Exegetical Commentary on the Epistle to the Romans Vol. II* (Edinburgh: T&T Clark, 1981), 595.

19 Lehman, *Ethics*, 238.

20 Philip Ziegler, 'Discipleship', in Kent Eilers and Kyle Strobel (eds), *Sanctified by Grace: A Theology of the Christian Life* (London: Bloomsbury/T&T Clark, 2014), 174.

21 Ziegler, 'Discipleship', 180.

22 John Webster, 'Confession and Confessions' in his *Confessing God: Essays in Christian Dogmatics II* (London: T&T Clark, 2005), 71.

23 Frances Young, *The Making of the Creeds* (London: SCM, 2002), 12.

24 As Jaroslav Pelikan put it, 'creeds and confessions will serve as the criterion for determining what true orthodoxy in doctrine is'. See his *Credo: Historical and Theological Guide to Creeds and Confessions of Faith in the Christian Tradition* (New Haven: Yale University Press, 2003), 77.

25 Philip Turner, 'Introduction' in Christopher Seitz (ed.), *Nicene Christianity: The Future for a New Ecumenism* (Grand Rapids: Brazos, 2001), 14.

26 Pelikan, *Credo*, 142.

# 2

# 'We Believe in God':
# Community and Morality

When the bishops gathered at Nicaea on 20 May in the year 325 there had never before been an ecumenical council. It was certainly expected and traditional for bishops to meet regionally to discuss and deliberate on matters affecting the churches under their oversight and care. On occasion they addressed theological matters of significance within the regions. But never had a Great Council been called to deliberate on a matter of importance to the Church universal. The invitation was sent to all bishops within the Roman Empire (and drew in several others who were outside of it), and was issued by the newly converted emperor, Constantine. He urged that the bishops 'promptly assemble' and that 'without delay in anything, speedily come ... in person' to contribute.[1] Of course, such an invitation attracted an unprecedented attendance from the bishops, despite the fairly treacherous journey for many of them, and there was significant geographical diversity too. Of the roughly 1,800 bishops who were invited, about 300 were present for the opening ceremony presided over by the Emperor and at which he personally welcomed those who had suffered persecution for their faith.

## Politics and Division

The urgency and imperial pomp was ostensibly due to division which had been wrought by a disagreement between Alexander, Bishop of Alexandria, and one of his senior priests, Arius, over the relationship between the person of Jesus Christ and God the Father, and therefore over the meaning of the Church's teaching on the Trinity. Arius, who had been a theological student of Lucian of Antioch, was, five years earlier, charged by Bishop Alexander with heresy for preaching an essential distinction between the Son of God and God, and which therefore suggested that Jesus Christ was not fully divine. In particular Arius claimed that if the Son is begotten of the Father, then the Son has a beginning and does not share in the Father's eternal nature. He put it to the bishop in a letter: 'the Father did not, in giving to Him [the Son] the inheritance of all things, deprive himself of what He has ingenerately in Himself; for He is the fountain of all things ... but the Son ... was not before His generation ... for He is not eternal or co-eternal or co-unoriginate with the Father ...'[2] Moreover, Arius rather mischievously claimed that he learned this from the bishop himself in Alexandria.[3] Alexander's response was necessarily tough, because he regarded Arius' position as compromising the means by which salvation and grace could be offered to the world – the biblical witness that only God saves (e.g. Ps. 62.5–8) – and, most importantly, ignoring what he thought was clear Apostolic teaching. Alexander sent a circular letter to his priests and fellow bishops accusing Arius and his supporters of a false and one-sided reading of the scriptures: 'They cry down all pious apostolic doctrine ... they deny His divinity and declare Him to be on a level with all mankind. They pick out every saying relative to His saving dispensation ... and try to compound from them the proclamation of their own impiety by abandoning the words showing His divinity from the beginning and His ineffable glory with the Father'.[4] In the year 320 Alexander summoned a local synod of the Egyptian and Libyan bishops where, following much deliberation, Arius was excommunicated and deposed from his church. Far from settling the matter, things got worse in the years that followed. Arius went to Caesarea and garnered the support of Bishop Eusebius (a fellow student of Lucian of Antioch), and then further to the eastern imperial capital of Nicomedia where its bishop, another Eusebius, offered his support. The Church was split, as bishops openly opposed one another (and bishops of the traditionally Apostolic Sees – those that had been founded by one of the original twelve – which was a significant problem in a culture where history and tradition mattered). It was at this point of episcopal stalemate that the issue probably came to the attention of the Emperor.

Constantine had only very recently been converted to Christianity (319), and even more recently had he become the sole Roman Emperor rather than the western Augustus (324). It came at a time of prolonged tribulation across the Empire, following its division into Tetrarchy after the resignation of Diocletian in the year 305, and the subsequent failure of co-operation between the leaders of the East and West. The final conflict between the two Augustuses followed a period of heightened suspicion on the part of the pagan Augustus Licinius, who feared Constantine's ambition and thought his conversion would inspire the Christians of the eastern empire to enact a *coup* to unify the empire under a Christian emperor. While there's little evidence that exactly this happened, it is interesting that when Constantine defeated Licinius to become the sole Emperor and thus unite East and West, he immediately set about constructing a new, overtly Christian, Imperial City to replace Nicomedia: Constantinople. Clearly his hope was that the Church might be a spiritual and religious agent for unification. Indeed, Constantine stated as much when he dispatched one of his trusted advisers, Ossius, Bishop of Cordoba, to attempt to reconcile Bishop Alexander and Arius in the year 324, writing that 'if I should succeed in establishing, according to my wishes, a common harmony of sentiment among all the servants of God, the general course of affairs would also experience a change ...'[5] He envisaged a consolidating and unifying role for the Church and its bishops, for which, however, the Church itself would need to be consolidated and unified. Constantine's imperial greeting at the opening of the Council of Nicaea therefore 'urged the bishops to achieve unity and peace'[6] with the expectation that 'the churches support order in the empire.'[7]

## Seeking the Truth Together

Though the threat of division may have been the wider political significance of the Council, its ecclesiastical significance was quite different. The bishops who gathered were principally concerned with questions of truth and the proclamation of the gospel, as the very few records of the event suggest.[8] Put positively, this meant that the Ecumenical Council aimed at unifying the Church's common understanding and thus proclamation, and therefore to put its house in order over the dispute between the divergent bishops (especially those from Apostolic Sees). Put negatively, this meant a deliberate restriction of belief and a move away from diverse opinions on some core matters and a growing willingness to exclude and excommunicate those who refused to cohere. And for precisely these reasons, the business of the Council really was the work of the bishops rather than Constantine. The Emperor was present to welcome the bishops to this new type of convocation, and he hosted a feast for its ultimate close in August 325, but 'he did not take part in the daily discussion nor did he vote on any issue. He considered his task to make sure the Council got the job done.'[9] During the first month of its meeting he heard regular updates and briefings and would attend and observe discussions, but it was the bishops who did the theological work and not the emperor. This followed the procedures of the Roman Senate, where the delegates were invited to contribute as they saw fit under the presidency of the emperor , but with the proviso that he would not interfere in the discussion. According to some scholars, this conciliar model actually 'enabled the Church to safeguard a certain independence in all matters of doctrine by encouraging the emperor to work through assemblies of bishops to achieve unity of belief'.[10] Crucially the Senate's conciliar method allowed for meaningful deliberation and discourse in an effort to discover the common mind of the gathered Council. The bishops were permitted to make proposals and reject alternatives. They were permitted to disagree, to argue, to persuade and to vote. This meant they were able to reach consensus, at least in theory, after considered theological debate. In an age in which the Church was dispersed and diverse, it mattered that there were common commitments.

Such a constructive climate was certainly not the product of politeness (as anyone familiar with the response of Nicholas, Bishop of Myra, to Arius will know).[11] Undoubtedly conciliar discussion and debate was already part of the Church's theological DNA, despite Nicaea being the first Council of such magnitude. For example, when a similar doctrinal disagreement arose about the means of salvation in the early Church, Paul and Barnabas were dispatched from the Church at Antioch to the Church at Jerusalem to meet with the elders. It began with a sharp dispute (Acts 15.2) between the Jerusalem missionaries and the Antiochene Christians over the need or otherwise for non-Jewish converts to Christianity to undergo circumcision, and in which Paul had taken a significant interest (cf. Gal. 3). The only resolution to this kind of theological problem was appeal to an apostolic council. The two Antiochene apostles were welcomed at Jerusalem, and after much discussion with the elders (Acts 15.6–7) in which no doubt the differing points of view were heard and debated in the light of Scripture and experience, the Jerusalem Council collectively resolved that indeed while it was not necessary to be circumcised, other aspects of moral conformity were essential for Christian converts (relating primarily to food and sex). This was then published as a letter from the *whole* Church at Jerusalem (15.22) to the church at Antioch and what seemed good to the Holy Spirit and the gathered Council was relayed to the co-believers (15.22–29). A collective decision had been reached. We might contrast this with another sharp disagreement later in the same chapter when Paul and Barnabas themselves argued about allowing John Mark to accompany them on their missionary journey (15.36–41). Here, the fierceness of the dispute meant that the same two apostles who had negotiated so well at Jerusalem then parted company (15.39). Interestingly, there's no recourse from either Paul or Barnabas to an apostolic council or any external authority to help them decide on John Mark's fate, nor to distinguish their competing apostolic wisdom. It was a different kind of argument. What was at stake was relatively insignificant and would not have affected the commonality of the Church's work and witness. It would not have compromised the essential meaning of the gospel to work with John Mark, though it might have negatively impacted its presentation among the gentiles because of his unreliability and history of desertion. Some things were worth a conciliar gathering and some were not. The biggest sign of the significance of both the subject matter discussed and the decisions reached by the Jerusalem Council was its ongoing status: Paul, having parted from Barnabas and been joined by Silas and Timothy, travelled throughout the regions of Cilicia and Lyconia and 'went from town to town [and] delivered to them for observance the decisions reached by the apostles and elders who were in Jerusalem' (Acts 16.4). They taught what the Council had decided, and though the Council was called to address the immediate disputants from Antioch and Jerusalem its ecumenical character can be seen in the wider promulgation of its decision. It was the same at Nicaea: the gathered Council made decisions about issues of gospel importance that not only addressed a dispute between Alexandria and Caesarea, but established the formal confessional boundaries of Christian orthodoxy thereafter because if they had not, the essential meaning of the Christian message would have been compromised.


## Corporate Deliberation?

There are few accounts of exactly how the Council of Nicaea worked out, but Bishop Eusebius of Caesarea helpfully described something of the decision-making process in a pastoral letter sent after its conclusion. He described elements of debate, discussion, disagreement and subsequent decision making and, though brief, it gives us some idea of the kind of exchange between delegates. In the first place, there were apparently several options presented to the Council for deliberation other than the final Creed that was promulgated. Eusebius related his own offering in the letter, a Caesarean Creed that was 'received from the Bishops who preceded us, and in our catechizings, and when we received baptism, and we learned from the divine Scriptures, and we constantly believed and taught as presbyter and bishop ... we now report to you ...'[12] It is interesting to see how he marshalled history, tradition and Scripture together here to establish his case before presenting anything of theological substance (this also allowed him to establish his own, and therefore also Arius', credentials). Eusebius then outlined a summary of the teaching of the churches under his episcopal oversight with direct quotations from Scripture (Col. 1.15; Matt. 28.19) to bolster its legitimacy. Eusebius then went on to explain how in the ensuing discussion other Nicene bishops offered additional texts, word, phrases and ideas that endorsed and expanded the Caesarean contribution rather than rejected it. On the use of the word *homoousios* (which describes the relationship between the Father and the Son as being of *one substance, homo-ousia*) Eusebius was quick to point out that he 'did not let it pass without inquiry in what sense they used the expression "of the substance of the Father"', and that 'accordingly, questions and explanations took place, and the discussion tested the meaning of the phrases'.[13] He was not alone in this; the bishops were generally allergic to any non-biblical language finding its way into their final document since anything a credal statement might have had to be contingent upon the prior authority of Scripture. It took weeks of debate and clarification of terms before they realized that an extra-biblical term that represented the essence of Scripture would be legitimate if carefully explained.[14] Eusebius offered the same scrutiny with the phrase 'begotten, not made' as well as the proposal to anathematize Arius' claim that 'before his generation, He was not' (though the latter was on the much less coherent basis that the Son of God obviously existed before His generation according to the flesh, demonstrating to some that Eusebius never really understood the seriousness of Arius' claim). Overall, the bishop was satisfied that the meaning of the Nicene Creed was acceptable to the theological standards of his own episcopal area and those of the other gathered bishops because it had been subjected to scrutiny and debate: 'all of us assented, not without inquiry, but according to the specific meanings mentioned before the religious Emperor himself and justified by the aforementioned considerations'.[15] The Council voted, and the Creed was eventually promulgated on 19 June in the year 325, mid-way through the Council.

That the substantial claims of the creed were agreed by majority is reflected in the use of the first-person-plural pronoun throughout, *pisteuomen – we believe*. But this was not simply the 'we' of the gathered bishops, it was an *ex officio* 'we' on behalf of the whole Church. The decision-makers were not simply speaking for themselves; the Council sought to represent all Christians everywhere. In the end, Arius and two other supporting bishops refused to acquiesce and were excommunicated. This was far more significant than the earlier excommunication by the Egyptian and Libyan bishops, when he could take refuge among the Caesarean and Nicomedian churches; there were very few options left to Arians after Nicaea. That the agreed promulgation of the Council was signed first by the Emperor's representative, Bishop Ossius, and then by the two Papal legates, and then the bishops of the eastern Apostolic Sees before finally all the other assenting bishops, was a clear indication of the universal status of the Creed. The 'we believe' points to the confessed faith of the Church universal which, it was hoped, would then be a 'touchstone by which the doctrines of the Church teachers and leaders might be certified as correct'.[16]

\*\*\*\*\*

## Communal Decision-Making

What might be implied for an ethics of Christian discipleship by this kind of conciliar thinking? Given that the basic function of a council is as a place of corporate deliberation and discourse, the obvious comparison is that just as the theological substance of the Church's faith and proclamation is a corporate project (albeit a contingent one) so too is the moral life of the Church and its members. As one commentator has put it, 'the contents of the devout and holy life are not a matter of personal taste for Christians'.[17] There is a collective dimension to ethical reasoning which we see again and again in St Paul's admonitions and challenges to the church communities: 'do nothing out of selfish ambition … but regard others as better than yourselves' (Phil. 2.3); 'each of us must please our neighbour for the good purpose of building up our neighbour' (Rom. 15.2); 'bear with one another, and if anyone has a complaint against another, forgive each other' (Col. 3.13); 'we hear that some are living in idleness, mere busybodies not doing any work … we command and exhort them … do work and earn a living' (2 Thess. 3.12). These references indicate that the biblical understanding of Christian community is all encompassing; not only were Christians bound to one another through common *beliefs*, but also through the outworking of those beliefs in common *decisions* and *actions*. This is grounded in fictive kinship which is a direct result of the saving work of Christ, i.e. that members of the church community are also brothers and sisters within the household of God. St Paul deployed these ideas 'to promote the solidarity and mutual regard among members of the congregations'[18] and thus to ensure the collective moral and spiritual health of the whole body. We see the same desire interwoven with his body-ecclesiology: 'just as the body is one and has many members … so it is with Christ … in the one Spirit we were all baptized into the one body … if any one member suffers, all suffer together; if one member is honoured, all rejoice with it … you are the body of Christ and individually members of it' (1 Cor. 12.12–

26). Moreover, such mutual regard and commonality was not to be limited to the localized congregations but extended to the universal body of Christ, the *koinonia* or *fellowship* of believers (cf. Acts 2.42-7), most especially those who were persecuted for the faith (cf. Rom. 15.26; 1 Cor. 16.1-4).

## Challenging Individualism

Such collectivism stands in sharp contrast to the individualism of contemporary western culture, with its turn towards self-fulfilment and self-authentication and away from external forms of meaning and purpose. The phenomenon has been discussed widely by sociologists since the second world war and increasingly by psychologists since the 1980s, and has its intellectual origins in the Enlightenment.[19] Rene Descartes' rationalistic turn to the 'self' was perceived as a great act of liberation because by it the problems associated with competing religious authorities – most notably warfare – could be overcome by simply refusing to concede the meaning of human life to any external power whatsoever, whether political, social or religious. By this the moral horizon was transformed, and so also the sense of what was possible. The story goes that the pursuit of self-fulfilment enabled freedom from historic oppressive structures shaped around status, class, gender, ethnicity, education, sexuality and wealth, 'from which it was once unthinkable to deviate' and liberated individuals (and therefore whole societies) to pursue the all-encompassing life-project that is self-determined existence.[20] A personal hallmark of this is that 'being true to myself means being true to my own originality [which] is something only I can articulate and discover … I am defining myself'.[21] With it comes the detachment of identity and meaning from community; in the individualist paradigm it is nearly impossible to make sense of my life outside of myself. I therefore need others not in order to understand myself, but only as and when they're necessary to achieve the fulfilment of self's re-envisioning.[22]

What has reasonably followed in the years since, according

to political philosopher Charles Taylor, is an approach to value and worth that focuses on maximum efficiency, i.e. that makes the value of something directly related to its significance for my life-project and the efficiency with which it helps me achieve my goals. This is a bi-product of an understanding of and approach to self-fulfilment that has been tinged with egoism.[23] In such a culture, realism is dead; human beings are free to redesign the world and its contents as they wish, as long as some basic reciprocal courtesies are observed. One such courtesy is the harm principle: 'the purpose for which power can be rightfully exercised over any member of a civilized community against his will is to prevent harm to others'.[24] The inverse of this principle is a modern cultural tag-line: do whatever you wish as long as you don't hurt anyone. (Interestingly, as a motto for modern progression, it often fails: one recent study argued that overtly individualistic cultures evidence greater levels of bad behaviour, deviance and delinquency among young adults because of the detachment from collective ideals such as community and responsibility.)[25] While it seems to be expansive, this approach to moral reasoning is actually quite narrowing. Universal agreement on what counts as 'harm' and knowing what actions are more harmful than others may sound like common sense, but it has actually been tricky to find consensus. Consider, for example, the competing interests of business and social welfare in western political discourse since the 1940s,[26] and the way this has been instrumental in making possible disasters such as the Grenfell Tower fire.[27] Individualism's aversion to larger frameworks of meaning and its subservience to a self-centred meta-narrative results in the undermining of commonality, reducing society to a co-existence of individuals pursuing their own ends within an agreed legal framework. Christian moral reasoning simply will not work in this space because it grows out of a corporate identity as Church, and therefore a common vision for what it means to live well before God. This suggests something necessarily mutual, collectivist and holistic which refuses individualism.

## Radner's Critique of Conciliarity

But we might wonder whether conciliarity inspired by the bishops of Nicaea is the best way for the Church to enact and maintain its community. In a potent analysis of the successes and failures of councils in the history of the Church, Ephraim Radner has argued that it is difficult and complicated to simply trust majority decisions as indicative of what is right. To do so would be akin to mob-rule. The tendency of those advocating for conciliarity has been to argue that the work of the Holy Spirit is central to the *mystery* of democratic and conciliar decision-making, often relying on Acts 15.28 to prove the point. But Radner cautions that such conflation is dangerous. This is because, theologically speaking, 'councils themselves are neither guaranteed pneumatic direction, nor does history convince us that many received it'.[28] His point is that the pursuit of consensus is not the equivalence of truthfulness; after all, the road that leads to destruction is broad (Matt. 7.13). Radner asks, 'was it not a "church council" that condemned Jesus to death?'[29] The question isn't meant to be flippant; it demonstrates that the mechanisms and processes of conciliarity are not enough to ensure right understanding and therefore right action. Consensus is not axiomatically Spiritual and may not even be possible: 'if the Spirit is known by its fruits … then pneumatic agreement is at best rare … or perhaps not even an historical existent except as a scriptural ideal'.[30]

Indeed, we might regard this idealized consensus-thinking as a strange commitment for the Church in the light of the Scripture where those who are gifted by the Spirit to speak the truth are often as far away from the collective as possible, operating on the edges of society and not at its centre: prophets. Interestingly, Radner grounds this critique within the Jerusalem narrative too, where, despite the conciliar nature of the apostolic meeting, it's what seemed good to the Holy Spirit (and thus derivatively to the elders and apostles) that was promulgated around the churches (Acts 15.28; 16.4). He calls this 'pneumatic instrumentality'[31] and it was what made all the difference, rather than the well-ordered discussion or mutual exchange or the art of persuasion leading to common thinking. We might guess on this basis that some form of spiritual discernment occurred at the Jerusalem gathering as well as debate and discussion – perhaps prayer and contemplation or a celebration of the Eucharist – and, moreover, that this was part of the decision-making process. Some have argued that the mutual agreement itself was the sign that the Spirit was present. But whatever it was, it is clear also that the Holy Spirit's leading was tangible to all who were present. To assume that councils naturally get things right and will always do so is to miss the independence of the Spirit's work and the necessity of proper discernment of the truth and to fail to reckon with the times Church councils get it wrong.

Radner develops the point about failure further using the work of historian Ramsay MacMullen.[32] MacMullen has argued that the strengths attributed to conciliar decision-making may be summarized under three aspects: cognitive, supernatural and democratic. These represent the serious beliefs of the early bishops of the church that: (1) it is possible to discern and apprehend the truth, and thus to know what is right; (2) such apprehension is the work of the Holy Spirit, and thus the truth that may be known and actually is known and promulgated is *divine* truth; (3) it is possible to know that it is the work of the Spirit and that what is believed is divine truth precisely because of the common discernment of the Council's delegates. But MacMullen also makes clear that each of these motivations has a shadow-side that has been equally present in the history of councils. The cognitive point can easily become a dangerously emotive one using inflammatory rhetoric, and often leading to violence; the supernatural point about the direct influence of the Holy Spirit has very quickly been used to demonize dissenters and to make enemies of those who ask questions; and the democratic point has been all too easily transformed into the demand for assent, however coercively attained.[33] It is not something that Christians have overlooked, but Radner suggests it is often explained away with a turn to providence – 'God makes use of fallen human beings in his Church to bring about good ends' – with the benefit of hindsight. Alas, Radner points out, this doesn't offer much help to, for example, those who suffer in places like Rwanda, where the majority Christian Hutu Tribe were responsible for the murder of nearly one million Tutsi in 1994.[34] If Christian ethics may learn anything from the Council of Nicaea, it must do so with concerns about its limitations and proper openness to dissenting voices at the front of its mind.

## The Way Ahead: Christian Commonality

What then are we to do about the Church's corporate project of deliberation today? It seems patently silly to suggest that seeking mutual counsel and engaging in discussion and debate on moral issues is not worth it, even if we agree with Radner's assessment of its limitations. If anything, it seems more important to take counsel together and not less if we are to effectively address the difficult decisions facing the Church and the various denominations within it today. Rather we should approach the task with a more sober account of the potential of corporate decision-making and a firmer grasp of what is necessary to best facilitate openness to the Holy Spirit's guidance. In Radner's discussion of the Council of Jerusalem, he argues that what enabled the success of the meeting (aside from the work of the Holy Spirit in bringing about its substantive conclusion) was, practically speaking, the quality of relationships between the churches 'built around practices such as regular gathering, devotion and submission to an apostolic centre of teaching, the sharing of the Eucharist, persistent prayer together, and the sharing of property. Only *out* of this comes one mind and one heart.'[35] These existing activities represented and enacted their common identity as followers of Jesus, and kept the gathering open to the work of the Spirit among them, while allowing for difference and disagreement. They were generous. Paul and Barnabas and James and the elders were already sisters and brothers in the faith; they were already fellow-worshippers and co-communicants; they already held their possessions in common and prayed for each other regularly. Their mutual attention to Christ did not immediately rub out their very real divergences, and neither did their divergences give them permission immediately to break fellowship with one another. In fact, their common commitment to Christ was the impetus to pursue a *consensus fidelium*. We may say something similar about Nicaea; that there was an Ecumenical Council that was well-attended, and that Constantine's administration knew who to invite to it indicates that, within reason, there was a desire for theological and ecclesial mutuality, and that the bishops were known to one another. Christian commonality is always prior to conciliarity, whether the latter is gathered formally or informally. Therefore, in the very least, maintaining common bonds of peace in Christ is necessary. It is community extrinsically grounded in devotion to Jesus Christ, rather than doctrinal purity, and is, therefore, the work of the Spirit of Christ, not the work of the gathered individuals in and of themselves. Or, as Dietrich Bonhoeffer eloquently put it, 'Christian community means community through Jesus Christ ... whether it be a brief, single encounter or the daily community of many years, Christian community is solely this: we belong to one another only through and in Jesus Christ.'[36] To meet together in council is to meet, discuss, as well as to *argue* and *debate* with other members of the household of God. Conciliarity is, therefore, the Church performing a specific task with a specific mode of reasoning, discourse and debate for the sake of the health of the whole. It is not to make us less devoted to Christ by sidelining our differences.

## The Way Ahead: Posture not Process

How, then, are we to maintain bonds of peace in a context where the Church's catholicity does not seem universal but fragmented, where there are over two billion people worldwide that identify as Christian, and where the World Council of Churches alone represents over 350 different denominations in over 150 countries? And further, in a context where there is considerable international divergence on significant ethical issues between churches and denominations? We might only think of two complex issues in one church, for example, the ordination of women and same-sex marriage in the Church of England, and we can begin to imagine the problems and complications of fruitful discourse. In a very helpful treatise on Christian community, the twentieth-century Christian martyr, Dietrich Bonhoeffer, advises that two things in particular will help with meaningful deliberation in a challenging ecclesial context, whether local, national or international. His advice pertains more readily to posture and attitude than it does to processes or structures. First, that Christians invest in the practices that bind us to one another by binding us to Jesus Christ, namely prayer and worship, and especially Holy Communion. This is true because 'without Christ we could not know other Christians around us, nor could we approach them because the way to them is blocked by one's own ego'. True worship is always disruptive of our own agendas and disagreements as it turns our attention to Jesus Christ in Word and Sacrament.[37] Second, Bonhoeffer encourages Christians to adopt a posture of service towards one another for the sake of obedience to Christ's call to love. The point is not to shift focus from Jesus to 'the other', but to see the value and worth of others precisely because we are orientated towards Jesus Christ. In serving others, Christians serve Christ.

A posture of service is key to fruitful deliberation because, according to Bonhoeffer, it is enacted in three particular ways within the life of a community. First, service means attentive *listening* to others in community in order to really inhabit their perspective for a while, even if ultimately you disagree. Listening of this sort means openness to hearing the Word of God from an unlikely source, but never from an enemy: 'those who can no longer listen to one another can no longer listen to God either.'[38] Listening is the necessary first step in any deliberation or debate because it allows us to apprehend what is going on, how others might see the situation, and what theological understanding they may have to offer. It helps us to understand what we're agreeing or disagreeing about, and brings clarity to our theological discourse. Listening is reciprocal, but only when listening is done does speaking begin. Listening is an active kind of attention, affirming the love of God for the other by turning ourselves towards the other in loving attention. Listening does not mean acquiescing, and it does not mean that disagreement is disallowed, but it does mean taking leave of your own voice to allow room for another's for a while. Second, service means *humility*. Bonhoeffer is quite direct about this, saying, 'we must be ready to allow ourselves to be interrupted by God, who will thwart our plans and frustrate our ways time and again, even daily, by sending people across our path with their demands and requests.'[39] To refuse to help or work with those whom God sends to disrupt our lives – perhaps those who also worship Jesus Christ but whom we think have somehow got their theology wrong – is to fail in the 'school of humility'[40] in which we have been enrolled by the Holy Spirit. Humility means refusing to take ourselves too seriously, and trusting that the Church is not an ideal for which we are responsible and therefore have to protect, but is a reality established and maintained by God and in which we participate – sometimes badly. Humility means time spent (maybe even time wasted from a human perspective) discerning the presence of God in a difficult conversation or argument or debate or discussion, and trying to see God's way forward for self and for others. Humility is a posture that we first develop in relation to God, and for whose sake we maintain it in relation to others. Humility is, therefore, a necessary kind of work, rather than an optional extra. Third, Bonhoeffer argues that service necessarily involves forbearance, and this is most naturally to be offered to one another within the household of God. The people we live with and should be closest to are often the ones who can most disrupt, annoy and irritate us. Bonhoeffer cites St Paul's command in Galatians 6.2, and then comments, 'the other person never becomes a burden at all for pagans, they simply stay clear of every burden the other person may create for them. However, Christians *must* bear the burden of another ... and by virtue of the law of Christ having been fulfilled, they *are* able to bear one another.'[41] To work with others is often tricky, especially where deliberation means conflict and disagreement and one's conscience is pricked about weighty matters of truth and the gospel. To forbear is to maintain fellowship as long as possible rather than break it at the first opportunity. To forbear is not simply to tolerate; as Bonhoeffer comments, reflecting on Isaiah 53.4–5, the work of Christ on the cross is the absolute work of forbearance, and through it is achieved the reconciliation and redemption of a whole community. Forbearance is costly and painful, but has the potential to be redemptive. To forbear is to listen, in humility, and to persevere with despite the significant differences that may perpetuate between people and it is at the heart of what a community does when it thinks together about difficult ethical issues.

Though these three – listening, humility and forbearance – are relatable in a variety of community contexts, I have drawn on them here as a means of navigating the complexity of conciliar and corporate reasoning by attending to the attitudes and posture that are necessary. I think this is more challenging than attending to the structures, processes and mechanisms that will also be important. The posture we adopt towards one another can be aggressive or welcoming, and this will shape the kinds of processes we're willing to engage with. It's not necessary to agree or to police someone's orthodoxy before we treat them well: it is necessary to remember that Christ loves them, and that is why prayer and worship are the starting point in Bonhoeffer's thinking. His idea of service takes seriously the preceding ideas that collective reasoning is a meaningful part of the Christian tradition from New Testament times, and suggests, I think, a way of maintaining conciliarity in ethical discourse that can be useful in a fractured and divided context such as ours today. It does not say much about process precisely because that must be agreed by those gathered, but it gestures toward the kind of relationships that make it possible to say 'we believe' in an honest, fruitful and constructive way by hearing one another and in so doing hearing the Holy Spirit.

## Questions

What do you think are the defining aspects of Christian faith, and how do these help us work with Christians from different backgrounds and traditions?

Do you think it might be possible for the Church to be an ethically diverse community? How, and why?

What is your attitude to Christians from traditions other than your own? What does it mean to think of them as co-believers?

## Further Reading

Bonhoeffer, Dietrich, *Life Together*, Dietrich Bonhoeffer Works, Vol. 5 (Augsburg. Fortress, 2005).

Root, Michael and James Buckley (eds), *The Morally Divided Body: Ethical Disagreement and the Disunity of the Church* (Eugene, OR: Cascade, 2012).

### Notes

1 'Constantine Summons the Council of Nicaea', in J. Stevenson (ed.), *A New Eusebius: Documents Illustrative of the History of the Church to AD 337* (London: SPCK, 1980), 358.

2 'Letter of Arius to Alexander, Bishop of Alexandria c.320', in Stevenson, *New Eusebius*, 346.

3 'Letter of Arius to Alexander, Bishop of Alexandria c.320', in Stevenson, *New Eusebius*, 347.

4 'The Arian Strategy According to Alexander of Alexandria, c.324', in Stevenson, *New Eusebius*, 348.

5 'The Mission of Ossius: Constantine's Letter to Alexander and Arius, 324', in Stevenson, *New Eusebius*, 352.

6 Henry Chadwick, *The Early Church* (London: Penguin, 1993), 130.

7 Joseph F. Kelly, *The Ecumenical Councils of the Catholic Church: A History* (Collegeville, MN: Michael Glazier/Liturgical Press, 2009), 17.

8 The great patristic scholar J. N. D. Kelly describes the lack of information about the Council's discussions as 'bafflingly obscure' when compared with the later Ecumenical Councils. But it may be precisely because Nicaea was the first that the problem arose. See his *Early Christian Creeds* (London: Longmans, Green and Co, 1950).

9 Kelly, *Ecumenical Councils*, 21.

10 Leo Donald Davis, *The First Seven Ecumenical Councils 325–787: Their History and Theology* (Collegeville, MN: Michael Glazier/Liturgical Press, 1990), 57.

11 According to legend, Bishop Nicholas lost his temper with the Aryans and punched one of them in the face. For his trouble he was stripped of his episcopal pallium, removed from the meetings, and imprisoned until the end of the Council by the other bishops who were appalled by his behaviour. Later legend says the Blessed Virgin Mary appeared to him in his cell and returned his pallium as a sign that she approved of his stance against heresy. Interestingly, this is not the thing for which Bishop Nicholas, later St Nicholas, is most famous: he was known as a very generous Bishop who gave gifts to poor children to celebrate Christ's nativity. Today he is known as Father Christmas.

12 'Letter of Eusebius of Caesarea to his Church on the Creed of Nicaea, 325', in Stevenson, *New Eusebius*, 365.

13 'Letter of Eusebius of Caesarea to his Church on the Creed of Nicaea, 325', in Stevenson, *New Eusebius*, 366.

14 Kelly, *Ecumenical Councils*, 24.

15 'Letter of Eusebius of Caesarea to his Church on the Creed of Nicaea, 325', in Stevenson, *New Eusebius*, 367.

16 Kelly, *Early Christian Creeds*, 205.

17 Philip Turner, *Christian Ethics and the Church: Ecclesial*

*Foundations for Moral Thought and Practice* (Grand Rapids: Baker Academic, 2015), 179.

18 David G. Horrell, *The Making of Christian Morality: Reading Paul in Ancient and Modern Contexts* (Grand Rapids: Eerdmans, 2019), 85.

19 See Cigdem Kagitcibasi, 'Individualism and Collectivism', in John Berry et al. (eds), *Handbook of Cross-Cultural Psychology, Vol. 3: Social Behaviour and Applications* (Boston, MA: Allyn and Bacon, 1997), 1–50. On the idea that Individualism is fast becoming a global phenomenon and not simply a western cultural trope as was once thought, see Takeshi Hamamura, 'Are Cultures Becoming Individualistic?', in *Personality and Social Psychology Review* Vol. 16.1 (2012), 3–24.

20 Charles Taylor, *The Ethics of Authenticity* (Cambridge, MA: Harvard University Press, 2003), 5. Though it is important to say that Taylor sees the pursuit of self-fulfilment as key to self-authentication, which is a potential virtue. It goes wrong, he argues, when it becomes self-indulgent. And it often does. See 71ff.

21 Charles Taylor, *Ethics of Authenticity*, 29.

22 Paul Ricoeur plots this development in terms of hermeneutics and post-Enlightenment culture as a two-fold process, wherein the act of interpretation is centred entirely on the subject. First it is centralized and 'de-regionalized', meaning that there are no local forms or contexts of interpretation; before second being 'radicalized' by separation of the epistemological ends of interpretation from the ontology of the knower. What matters in such an environment is the universalized knowing subject, not the act of knowing and what may be appropriate to it. See Ricoeur, 'The Task of Hermeneutics' in his *Hermeneutics and the Human Sciences: Essays Language, Action and Interpretation* (Cambridge: Cambridge University Press, 1981), 3–22.

23 Taylor, *Ethics of Authenticity*, 71.

24 John Stuart Mill, *On Liberty* (New York: Appleton-Century Crofts, 1947), 9.

25 Marijana Kotlaja, 'Cultural Contexts of Individualism vs. Collectivism: Exploring the Relationships between Family Bonding, Supervision and Deviance', in *European Journal of Criminology* (2018).

26 See, for example, the very helpful summary article by Patricia Smith, 'Individualism and Social Responsibility: Reflections on Recent Work by French and May', in *Social Theory and Practice* Vol. 20.3 (1994), 363–80.

27 For a cogent analysis of this see Maya Goodfellow, 'Grenfell will Force Britain to Confront its Greatest Failure' in *Prospect*, 14 July

2017,www.prospectmagazine.co.uk/magazine/grenfell-will-force-britain-to-confront-its-greatest-failure (accessed January 2019).

28 Ephraim Radner, *Brutal Unity: The Spiritual Politics of the Christian Church* (Waco, TX: Baylor University Press, 2012), 242.

29 Radner, *Brutal Unity*, 242.

30 Radner, *Brutal Unity*, 247.

31 Radner, *Brutal Unity*, 222.

32 Ramsay MacMullen, *Voting About God in Early Church Councils* (New Haven: Yale University Press, 2006).

33 Radner, *Brutal Unity*, 243–4.

34 Radner cites this in *Brutal Unity*, 29–39. For a challenging and hopeful account of what followed from Rwanda see Denise Uwimana, *From Red Earth: A Rwandan Story of Healing and Forgiveness* (Robertsbridge: Plough Publishing, 2019).

35 Radner, *Brutal Unity*, 173–4.

36 Dietrich Bonhoeffer, *Life Together*, Dietrich Bonhoeffer Works Vol. 5 (Augsburg: Fortress, 2005), 31.

37 Bonhoeffer, *Life Together*, 33.

38 Bonhoeffer, *Life Together*, 98.

39 Bonhoeffer, *Life Together*, 99.

40 Bonhoeffer, *Life Together*, 100.

41 Bonhoeffer, *Life Together*, 101.

# 3

# 'Maker of Heaven and Earth': Consuming Our Fellow Creatures

It has been quite common, especially in the last 25 years, to consider the doctrine of creation – denoted in the Nicene Creed with the phrase 'maker of heaven and earth' – within the field of Christian apologetics. This is almost entirely as a response to the post-Darwinian new-atheist movement headed by natural scientists like Richard Dawkins and Sam Harris, philosophers such as Daniel Dennett, and public intellectuals such as Christopher Hitchens, whose approach has been aggressive in its disdain for religious accounts of reality.[1] Many Christian scientists have ventured to engage in the debate, including biophysicist and theologian Alister McGrath and physicist and Anglican priest John Polkinghorne. They have made their responses on both scientific and philosophical grounds, i.e. as scientific peers and as Christians.[2] What is evident from the ongoing discourse is the paucity of understanding of the meaning of the Christian doctrine of creation by those who criticize it. What is misunderstood is that the doctrine of creation does not intend to be an account of *how* things came to be, rather it describes *why* things came to be. It suggests that there is a creative force behind or prior to that of evolution, and that this is where meaning and purpose originate: God. The critics have been quick to say that it is not necessary to attribute purpose to something once we know that it *originated* as a cosmic accident, and that the god-hypothesis that was relied upon by the ancients can now be dismissed as a sub-intellectual response to the conundrum of meaning. The debate rumbles on, though there are signs that western, liberal democracies are becoming impatient with the aggressiveness of new atheism even if such societies are not necessarily becoming more religious.[3]

I begin with this reference to the science/faith debate because in considering the implications of the doctrine of creation for an integrated ethics of discipleship I want to resist the temptation to focus on questions of process and mechanics and thereby overlook the theological substance – though I realize there may be some pressure to do the former and not the latter in the current climate. The form such resistance takes here is to prioritize the *confessional* nature of the doctrine, by which I mean prioritizing the fact that Christians regard creation *as creation* (i.e. as a reality that has a creator) on the basis of faith and therefore on the basis of revelation. Without such, creation would be something to experience and know about, but it wouldn't be *creation*. It would be nature. After all, the doctrine is a credal statement rather than a self-evident truth.[4] It is proclaimed in the Church's creeds because it is witnessed in Scripture, and not necessarily because modes of scientific reason can establish it. Further, this means that, as I suggested in chapter one, the idea that God is creator and human beings are creatures is a commitment that confers identity upon those who believe it; we are radically implicated as products of God's creative activity each time we confess it.

## Biblical Foundations

Like all good theology, the doctrine of creation has substantial scriptural antecedents. The psalmists' poetic celebration of divine creativity is powerful, 'you stretch out the heavens like a tent ... you make the clouds your chariot ... you set the earth on its foundation ... you cause the grass to grow for cattle and the plants for people to use ...' (Ps. 104), and the sensation that is elicited when humans pause to admire it draws us into the habit of awe and wonder, 'when I look to the heavens, the work of your hands, the moon and the stars which you have ordained, what is man that you are mindful of him?' (Ps. 8). Other texts consider the theology of divine sovereignty holding everything together, 'By the word of the LORD the heavens were made' (Ps. 33), and point to the underlying mystery that that suggests, 'where were you when I laid the foundation of the earth? ... Who determined its measurements ... or who laid its cornerstone when the morning stars sang together and all the heavenly beings shouted for joy?' (Job 38.4–7). Creation speaks of God's glory and calls human creatures into worship (Ps. 19), and how it might be the basis for some kinds of theological reasoning. But in terms of the substance of the doctrine of creation, the opening verses of Genesis give us the basic building blocks:

> In the beginning when God created the heavens and the earth, the earth was a formless void and darkness covered the face of the deep, while a wind from God swept over the face of the waters. Then God said, 'Let there be light'; and there was light. (Genesis 1.1–3)

Famous for its familiar clarity and directness, there are nonetheless some hermeneutical and exegetical difficulties in these few verses which reflect the complexity of the rest of Genesis (and the wider Pentateuch), and which are worthy of a little further reflection if we are to see some of the layers of meaning within the doctrine.[5] The issues relate specifically to the syntax of the passage and the relationships between each of the verses. How we deal with these will shape our wider theological understanding.

The rendering of these verses in the NRSV – 'when God created' – might suggest that at the point of God's creative work there was already some kind of existing material that was formless and void. The phrase 'in the beginning' would therefore relate to the point at which God started to work on the material rather than to the beginning of all things. In this reading, God fashions creation out of pre-existing chaos and gives it order and shape, imposing the divine will on to something that was hitherto meaningless. This view is strengthened when we read v. 1 in direct relation to the final verse of the narrative in 2.4a and thus as a chiastic structure where the key ideas develop across the whole narration in a symmetrical pattern (A,B,B,A). Such structures were typical of certain kinds of didactic material, often epic poetry, where the writer wanted to persuade the reader of a particular point of view. In this case, the chiasmus is short, 'God creates the heavens and earth (1.1)//the heavens and earth God created (2.4a)', and the in-between verses seek to persuade us of the chiasmus' central claim by offering supporting material. Thus what is enfolded within the opening and closing verses is explication, and what emerges is the view that God's creative activity is a 'a matter of organizing pre-existing chaos' by contrasting it with 'the dreadfulness of the situation before the divine word brought order out of chaos'.[6] It is a view often criticized for its implicit Hellenistic and gnostic dualism, where God the Spirit imposes order on to matter thereby overcoming it.[7] Though there is certainly some dualism here, it may not necessarily be Greek.

The Old Testament scholar Gerhard von Rad suggested that the dualism of the creation narrative is not that between spirit/matter, but between two versions of ourselves: 'Man has always suspected that behind all creation lies the abyss of formlessness ... that the chaos, therefore, signifies simply the threat to everything created ... thus [Genesis] speaks first of the formless and the abysmal out of which God's will lifted creation and above which it holds it unceasingly, as permanently in need of this supporting Creator's will.'[8] The text presents us with opposing versions of creatureliness, with and without God's word, and clarifies that only one of these is good. Creation is, therefore, not simply an event of the past in which God is defined in relation to what has happened, but a past-present-continuous activity in which God was and is and will be the one whom human beings need in order to be fully human.

But, equally, verses 1 and 2 might suggest that God's first activity was to make the formless void, and from this chaos God fashioned the rest of creation in an orderly manner. Such a reading might make sense of the text by treating the passage sequentially, so that verses 3 and onwards are there to elucidate the major theological claim of verses 1 and 2, so that we're intended to read it something like, 'God made the heavens and the earth by first creating a formless void, and then working on it over a period of six (figurative) days.' This is the traditional reading of the passage. But lurking within it is a bold theological statement: that God was the originator of the chaotic void in the first place. Two questions naturally follow this assertion: first, how it is possible for God, who is usually thought to be non-material, to create a material world? This is sometimes known as the problem of *emanation*, or the idea that everything that exists derives directly from God. It is not such a problem in the discussion above, because God is thought to be working and re-working what already exists, but it is problematic here when what God made was presented in only negative terms. Thus, second, it raises the question how is it possible for God to create something disordered and formless and void when in the rest of the Old Testament orderliness is celebrated and God is praised for the structures of creation (e.g. Ps. 19.1; Ps. 74.12–14; Isa. 45.18).

The first question 'presupposes the notion that the cause of the material world must be present in its effect …'[9] and this has usually been dealt with in a manner following St Augustine, who argued that creation is 'from God' (*de ipso*) but not 'of God' (*ex ipso*) and thus that matter comes from a matter-less God by virtue of God's sovereign freedom. More recently, however, subtler answers to this conundrum have been proposed, rooted in St Paul's bold claim that 'in Christ, all things in heaven and on earth were created' (Col. 1.16), and the similar sentiments of the Johannine prologue, 'all things came into being through him, and without him nothing came into being' (John 1.3), and the (deutero-Pauline) letter to the Ephesians where we see the radical claim that 'God the Father chose us in Christ before the foundation of the world' (Eph. 1.4).[10] In each, the person of Jesus Christ plays a significant role not only in making sense of what creation is, but in the very fact that creation is at all. Inherent in this is the idea that the doctrine of creation is not first and foremost about creatures, but about God. As Karl Barth has put it, 'the confession ... does not say 'I believe in the created world', nor even 'I believe in the work of creation'. But it says, 'I believe in God the creator'.[11] The emphasis on God has led theologians such as Kathryn Tanner and Rowan Williams to suggest that Trinitarian theology points to the *incarnation* as a better starting point for making sense of creation (thus reversing the usual paradigm where creation is taken as the benchmark for understanding the incarnation) since the precise conundrum of the relationship between creature and the Creator is enacted radically in the person of Jesus Christ.[12] Any meaningful connection between cause (God) and effect (creation) may only really be established in this singular divine-human.[13] Where Augustine emphasized divine power and sovereignty over creation, this latter view emphasizes God's determination over God's own life to be *for* creation in Christ, and thus starts with grace as the foundation of all that exists. Christ is the centre and meaning of the creation narrative, and the one towards whom creation is moving in its eschatological trajectory. Consider St Paul's words that 'all things will be subjected to him' (1 Cor. 15.28) or the new creation in John's Revelation with the throne of God is at its centre (Rev. 21.1–4). We might place these alongside Isaiah's eschatological picture of a peaceful kingdom, most often read at Christ's Nativity, in which creation is re-made and re-ordered by the one upon whom the Spirit of the Lord rests (Isa. 11.1–9; Luke 4.18) to see how Christ may be considered fulfilment as well as originator of creation.

The sharpness of the second question, about disorderliness and chaos as the work of God, is increased when we consider the negative attitude with which Genesis 1 regards the shapeless mess at the beginning compared to the daily refrain 'And God saw that it was good' celebrating each act of creation on subsequent days. Realization of this problem is perhaps why there have been so many efforts in the history of Christianity to insert a theological 'gap' between v. 1 – where God created the heavens and the earth, and the more challenging v. 2 – where what God made was formless and void. Christians have long puzzled over the incongruity between an all-powerful and good God, and the formlessness and apparent dysfunctionality of what was made. Perhaps, it is sometimes suggested, something happened between these two events of God creating and the earth becoming formless and void? Mythic cosmic battle ideologies produced by interpreting texts such as Isaiah 14.3–23 on the downfall of the king of Babylon as describing the fall of Lucifer (cf. Isa. 14.12) or supplementary 'angelic rebellion' narratives such as that in John Milton's *Paradise Lost* try to explain how the work of God in v. 1 could have become void in v. 2 (the effects of Lucifer's rebellion), leading to creation as demonstrating God's victory over the angelic rebels in v. 3 onwards. The aim is apologetic; the chaos is there to be sublimated by God. But the problem is obvious; it is not possible to explain the mystery of creation in this way without becoming speculative. We know about the beginning only because we receive it as revelation in the witness of Scripture, and what we know is that the beginning is God's work and understanding it is God's prerogative. Elsewhere the point is made explicit: 'Where were you when I laid the foundations of the earth? Tell me if you have understanding' (Job 38.4); 'O Lord, how manifold are your works! In wisdom you have made them all; the earth is full of you creatures' (Ps. 104.24); 'By faith we understand that the worlds were prepared by the word of God, so that what is seen was made from things that are not visible' (Heb. 11.3); 'You are worthy, Lord our God ... for you created all things, and by your will they existed and were created' (Rev. 4.11).

## Theological Considerations

Doctrine works by summarizing the scriptural witness; it is consistent with Scripture by saying what is basic to it and thus permitted by it rather than because it irons out all of the exegetical challenges. Doctrines give summative voice to the complexities of the Bible by 'distilling a complex set of exegetical judgements …'[14] Within the Genesis passage there are three salient points that can be observed for a theology of creation:

> What pervades in the whole narrative is the idea that God gives shape and order, and thus meaning, purpose and direction to all of creation: 'only in God is the universe a universe. But for him, it would fall away into chaos and confusion.'[15] Whether by re-ordering chaos or by birthing chaos as the first stage in the process of creation, it is God's will and action that is the first cause of all that we know as creation.
>
> There is a clear distinction to be made between Creator and creature, which reaches to the most fundamental levels of who we are and who God is – what we call *ontology*. God is un-originate and all powerful; creatures are contingent and externally determined. For creatures, meaning and purpose must be discerned rather than constructed; it is extrinsic rather than intrinsic. God is not like us but better; God is fundamentally different.
>
> Human beings are fellow creatures alongside non-human animals as well as all else that has come into being as God's work. This means that the divine determination is not simply for creation, but for a differentiated creation. Not all creatures are the same, nor do they have the same purpose, but creatureliness is shared and interlinked. We see this in the refrain of creation's 'goodness' prior to the existence of human beings. We must avoid anthropocentric (human-centred) accounts of the creation story. It is about God, and the goodness of God's work and only then is it about the place of human beings within that. Just as to consider the meaning and purpose of human life cannot be done in isolation from God, nor can it be done in isolation from fellow-creatures.

One final theological consideration about creation may be offered before moving to the ethical material. It has been the Church's tradition from the earliest days to articulate within the doctrine of creation a firm and clear account of *creation ex nihilo,* or 'creation from nothing'. This technical piece of theological reasoning is never really claimed outright by the biblical authors, though there may be some suggestions of it in Genesis and certainly examples littered throughout scriptures of the absolute and singular sovereignty of God directly related to creation (e.g. Ex. 20.11; Ps. 33.6; Ps. 102.25; Isa. 44.6, 24; John 1.3; Acts 17.24; Rom. 11.36; Col. 1.16; Rev. 4.11). Like the doctrine of the Trinity, it has significant biblical antecedents and is regarded by most as thoroughly biblical, but also like the doctrine of the Trinity it cannot be substantiated with a single proof-text.[16] As a formula, it comes from a second-century argument in which the then Bishop of Antioch, Theophilus, used the idea to explain something important about God's sovereign freedom. He wrote,

> How is it great if God made the universe out of pre-existing material? For a human craftsman, too, when he receives material from someone, makes from it whatever he wishes. But the power of God is made manifest in this: that he makes whatever he wishes out of whatever does not exist.[17]

The Bishop's concern was to protect the sovereignty of God from any pretenders, especially those who would read Genesis 1 as suggesting pre-existing material that had an alternative source of origin. For God to be *the* God and not *a* god, the doctrine of creation cannot admit another sovereign and generative being equal to God. His point was that 'God had no need to rely on anything outside of himself, and so creation is an act of divine sovereignty and freedom.'[18] Theophilus' intention caught on because of the force of its logicality, and became part of the Christian tradition (and in some cases a required statement of faith).[19] The point is that God was thus not compelled or forced to create, nor was he hindered in his own aseity or immanent life by creation or the act of creating. Rather God willed creation for its own sake: it neither adds to nor detracts from God's life.

Though some find this hard to hear pastorally, it really matters theologically: if God needs creatures to complete some sense of lack in God's own existence then it places a burden upon creatures and upon God to make the relationship work. It does not permit the possibility of creaturely failure. Creation could never be free, but would always be coerced into being the solution to God's personal crisis. Moreover, sin could never be dealt with properly: if creation's role were to top-up God's inadequacies then God would not have sufficient distance from creation to be the saviour creatures need. *Creatio ex nihilo* declares the opposite: that creation is not necessary. It is, rather, desired in freedom and love. Understood in this way, creation has the character of divine gift and this means it is, from its origin, graced. In theological terms, this brings us back to Christology: Jesus Christ is the one through whom the grace of God has come (John 1.17). This means the whole history of creation, from beginning to end, takes place under the sovereignty of God's will and desire for creatures rather than some necessity or requirement. God's commitment is, therefore, not coerced but chosen; creation's telos is established intentionally rather than arbitrarily. We might add, therefore, another salient point to those listed earlier on page 58: (4) Creation is because of God's grace and love, through which creatures have been brought into being and purposed to flourish as creatures, and this means finding their end-goal in God's will.

*****

Questions of meaning, purpose and direction are morally significant. They are bound up with the *telos* of particular creatures within the wider *telos* of God's creation. Knowing what something is *for* begins to suggest appropriate ways to engage with it and highlights ways of engagement that are inappropriate or even destructive. Scripture is surprisingly quiet on the question of why God created. It is clear that creation exists because of

God, but not so much about God's purpose and intention in creating in the first place, though some Christians thinkers have tried to surmise the divine purpose. For example, Thomas Aquinas argued that creation exists principally for humans to consume and enjoy as the final objects of God's desire, and therefore it may be used in whatever way necessary to achieve their happiness; Karl Barth argued that creation exists as a kind of stage or setting for the grand enactment of God's covenant with humanity, beyond which it has no meaning or purpose. There are other examples that follow a similar train of thought, and all reflect an inherent anthropocentrism. That means that they all make sense of non-human creation in direct relation to humanity. But this seems like a fundamental error, especially if the theological considerations outlined above are taken into account. In the Genesis narrative, human beings do not feature in the story of creation until day six, and yet on days one to five the work of God was celebrated as good. It received God's blessing and affirmation aside from its relation to humanity (Gen. 1.3–25). This is precisely because the proper orientation of non-human creation is the same as that of human beings, namely it is Godward facing. All creation exists because of God and for God (John 1.3; Col. 1.16). Thus, God gives meaning and purpose to all creatures, not simply humans, and that purpose existed before human beings. The value and worth of non-human animals is, therefore, established prior to the creation of human beings; they do not exist for us, but for God. This challenges any pretense toward anthropocentrism: 'the proper ends of human and non-human animals, and the proper relation between those ends, must be shaped by an understanding of God's good purposes …'[20] The natural question that flows from this is *what is God's purpose for non-human animals?*

David Clough's groundbreaking work in this area offers us help to make sense of the issues.[21] He turns to the theological substance of the doctrine of creation to subvert the notion that there may be hierarchy among the creatures of God – 'if we confess God as creator *ex nihilo* we must recognize that our basic relationship to creation is to recognize that we are part of it … this basic creaturely solidarity is between all things made by God …' – and in so doing he undermines any notion that human creatures may necessarily have a different *reason for being* or *telos* from non-human ones.[22] As the Genesis narrative reminds us, the goodness of creation is not its anthropocentric usefulness but its fulfilment of God's creative intention. Even without human beings it was still 'good'. Both human and non-human creation is the result of God's good pleasure and desire; God was not coerced into creating plants and animals because he had already created humans and needed to feed and house them. Neither were humans created because God was struggling to look after the plants and animals and wanted someone to tend creation. God was not forced to create to satisfy some external problem or a difficulty intrinsic to certain aspects of creation. Creation is an act wrought in freedom, and driven by divine will and desire. Clough summarizes, 'a Christian way of understanding the other animals that we live among is to recognize them as fellow animal creatures of the God we share, fellow recipients with us of God's grace in creation, reconciliation and redemption, willed by God to flourish and to glorify God in their flourishing'.[23] The driving force here is the grace of God, which is God's freedom. The abundance of this grace creates fellowship among its recipients. Any sense in which God was required to create anything at all leads to the undermining of grace and an undermining of the ensuing fellowship. Clough reminds us then that non-human animals are as much the result of this freedom as humans are. This is a subtle but significant shift; by remembering that the doctrine of creation is first and foremost about God rather than about creatures, Clough is able to overcome any sense that animals may be annexed and commercialized purely for the benefit of human beings. As St Paul proclaims, all creatures find their meaning and end in Christ (Col. 1.16). To flourish as a creature, and a non-human creature in particular, is to fulfil God's intention. Thus, the first ethical implication we might draw is to say that Christians must subvert anything that does not contribute the flourishing of non-human animals, and actively promote what does.

## The Flourishing of Non-human Animals?

What does flourishing mean for non-human animals? One area in which this question must be answered is the production and consumption of non-human animals for food. There are two aspects to this: the first considers whether Christians ought to eat meat at all; the second considers what methods of farming and cultivation are appropriate. It is difficult to separate the two, and even more difficult to consider them in the order here proposed. If we say that at least for now, while all of creation awaits the eschaton, it is appropriate for Christians to eat meat (even if we think in the coming Kingdom of God we'll all be vegetarian) then we must consider the question of production and habits of consumption. Assuming that we think that the way in which meat is produced matters, and the welfare of non-human animals is important to the God who created them, then unethically produced meat is unlikely to be acceptable for Christians. On the flip side, if the general patterns of meat production are seen to be without the standards of concern and wellbeing that are consistent with the doctrine of creation, it ought to mean that Christians reduce their meat consumption, find alternative sources of production, or opt for a plant-based diet. It is to this latter point that I turn in this section. I am here concerned with the methods of meat production and whether Christians can meaningfully participate in these as purchasers and consumers or whether a commitment to the mutual flourishing of human and non-human animals requires an alternative diet.

The history of mass consumption of non-human animals is relatively recent, and so with it both the processes and ethics of consumption have intensified and developed. As Clough narrates it,

the first large-scale rearing of farmed animals exclusively for meat was in England in the late eighteenth century: up to that point meat was largely a by-product of keeping animals for other reasons, such as milk, eggs and wool. Meat was a cash-crop made possible by the Highland clearances in Scotland and the enclosures in England, displacing the largely arable agriculture of the poor ...[24]

What has followed is two centuries of technological advancement to increase the yield and product, and to provide cheaper meat for sale. Tastes have changed; meat has become a significant ingredient in nearly every meal and the demand for it has increased. A recent study commissioned by the BBC stated that the average person in the UK consumes 75kg of meat per year, and that despite the fact that a social attitudes survey undertaken in 2016 showed that a third of UK adults had reduced their meat consumption or become vegetarian/vegan in the previous five years. The figures show a startling rise compared with a century ago.[25] The industry has been focused on its outputs, and thus its yield increases have relied upon treating non-human animals as a commodity to be exploited rather than fellow-creatures to be encouraged.

Clough gives the example of broiler hens reared in intensive conditions (as opposed to free-range or organic broilers) which are slaughtered at 35 days old. In such environments feeding is regulated and regimented to enable the hens to grow three times faster than they would in normal circumstances: the goal and expectation is massive weight gain in the quickest times possible to satisfy demand. The charity *Compassion in World Farming* estimates that the average broiler hen farmed in such conditions gains 50g in weight per day, and that 'over the last 80 years or so, the slaughter age of a standard fast growing broiler has been decreasing, and market weight has increased ...'[26] Such rapid growth means that many broiler hens in these conditions are reduced to sitting down all day because their legs do not develop at the same rate as their body mass and so are unable to support their own weight.[27] Many of the sheds within which these chickens are reared use artificial light to regulate the feeding times, and are prone to significant overcrowding. This leads the hens to become stressed and anxious, leading to feather loss and skin irritation. Over 70% of broiler hens, and therefore of the chicken available in supermarkets, are reared in these conditions.

Something similar can be said for pork. Over 1.4 billion pigs are slaughtered around the world each year, of which around 11 million are farmed in the UK. Like broiler hens, the majority are intensively farmed and are fed in such a way that they can be slaughtered from five months old, twice as fast as organic pigs left to grow at a more natural rate. Around 60% of sows in the UK give birth in farrowing crates, small metal cages in which the sows are contained on their sides to allow access for suckling piglets, which the RSPCA acknowledges 'prevent the sows from being able to turn around ... for up to five weeks ...'[28] Recent investigative journalism has shown that tail-docking (though not best practice according to the RSPCA) is quite common in industrial pig farming because the lack of space in the enclosure impacts the pigs mental health and wellbeing, causing them to become anxious and to bite one another's tails.[29] Pigs are social creatures, intensely curious and intelligent, but intensive farming requires large numbers to live in barns with slatted wooden floors in confined spaces often without straw, preventing them from foraging or wallowing. They have to sleep and defecate in the same space, which is unhygienic and unnatural when compared with pig behaviour in the wild. According to the RSPCA, pigs in this sort of environment become stressed and aggressive.[30]

We might also take the example, also cited by Clough, of commercial egg production. Around 24 million eggs are produced for the UK market each year, by 32 million hens. A consequence of mass production of eggs is the mass culling of male chicks. Chicks bred for eggs are of a different size and type from broiler hens, and obviously only the females are useful for laying. The males are of no use in meat production and therefore have no economic or gastronomic value. It is widely agreed that the most humane form of culling is maceration[31] within 15 minutes of hatching, though the *British Egg Information Service* has insisted that in UK male chicks are gassed within 24 hours of hatching.[32] All UK commercial egg production involves the destruction of male chicks as integral to the process.

It is hard to believe that such examples are really about the flourishing of the fellow-creature before God. Industrialized farming limits and distorts the lives of those creatures subjected to it, and makes destruction of life axiomatic. It is about the commodification of the animals involved, resulting in the diremption of the fellowship between them and human beings which is integral to the doctrine of creation. And while we might want to say that Christians should purchase meat from non-industrialized production-lines, the same charge of commodification and exploitation could be applied wherever non-human animals are treated as if they exist solely for human consumption rather than for their own flourishing. And all this seems to run contrary to the goal and vision of creation witnessed in Scripture and expressed within the doctrine. It is to Scripture that I want to turn again, before suggesting ethical actions that are implied by the doctrine of creation.

## The Peaceable Kingdom

When the doctrine of creation considers the meaning and purpose of creation, its *telos*, within the Christian tradition we are not simply looking backwards to what happened in the beginning, but forwards to the eschatological fulfilment of God's creative purpose. This is absolutely consistent with the theological considerations I discussed in the first part of this chapter; the purpose that will one day be revealed is that with which creation was imbued in the beginning, and only God knows it fully. Christian ethics discerns what creaturely flourishing might be by looking backwards *and* looking forwards, caught as it is between creation and the eschaton.

One of the most important prophetic visions of the coming Kingdom, in which the relationship between human and non-human animals is central and defining, is Isaiah's vision of the Peaceable Kingdom. It is a powerful picture of the fulfilment of God's plans and purposes for all of creation and provides 'a focal part of what it will mean for the righteousness of Yahweh to be realized on earth … [including] a new mode of existence between animal creatures will be inaugurated …'[33]

> The wolf shall lie down with the lamb,
> The leopard shall lie down with the kid,
> The calf, and the lion, and the fatling together,
> And a little child shall lead them.
> The cow and the bear shall graze
> Their young shall lie down together;
> And the lion shall eat straw like an ox.
> The nursing child shall play over the hole of an asp,
> And the weaned child shall put his hand on the adder's den.
> They will not destroy or hurt, on all my holy mountain …
> On the day, the root of Jesse shall stand as a signal to the peoples;
> The nations shall inquire of him and his dwelling place shall be glorious.
>
> (Isa. 11.6–10)

Of course, there is poetic license involved in a well-painted picture such as this, but its meaning is clear: in the coming Kingdom, what we currently regard as the natural habit of carnivores to eat other animals shall be sublimated. What might currently be dangerous situations for some, like the lamb alongside the wolf, are transformed into icons of freedom. Consumption will give way to mutuality, safety and peace. A new kind of diet and a new kind of fellowship will be established among creatures of all kinds. This certainly implies human as well as non-human animals, as the presence of the nursing and weaned children suggests. Isaiah's vision is that God's rule means a full re-ordering of the way things are between animals of all kinds. What makes this passage especially powerful for Christians is that it is preceded by Isaiah 11.1–5, one of the prophetic oracles of the Advent liturgy – the third 'O Antiphon' – which is said and sung to anticipate the birth of Jesus Christ. These antiphons have been in use during Advent since at least the eighth century.

> A shoot shall come out from the stump of Jesse,
> A branch shall grow out of his roots.
> The spirit of the Lord shall rest on him,
> The spirit of wisdom and understanding,
> The spirit of counsel and might,
> The spirit of knowledge and the fear of the LORD.
> His delight shall be in the fear of the LORD.
>
> He shall not judge by what his eyes see,
> Or decide by what his ears hear;
> But with righteousness he shall judge the poor,
> And decide with equity for the meek of the earth …
> (Isa. 11.1–5)

St Paul quotes the end of this oracle to summarize the hope that Jesus Christ brings (Rom. 15.12) and to link the long-hoped-for messianic figure with Jesus Christ. For Christians then, ethics should anticipate the coming Kingdom of Jesus by reasoning backwards from a vision of what that Kingdom will look like; one of creaturely harmony, mutuality and dignity before God, free from consumption and predatory relationships. To herald this Kingdom is the calling of all Christians, and this has implications for the way we live now.

## Be Creature Kind

Becoming vegetarian may not be a biblical necessity at present (after all, Jesus cooked and served fish after the resurrection, see John 21.9), but many Christians have argued that the failure of the production process to contribute to animal flourishing coupled with the eschatological vision of a peaceable Kingdom in which the predatory relationship between animals will be overcome means it should be a realistic implication of the doctrine of creation. Many have preferred plant-based diets in anticipation of the coming Kingdom – as a sign and herald of what will be, and a rebellion against the current situation. However we feel about meat-eating, if God's determination for non-human creation is that it should flourish for its own sake rather than being commodified for the supposed flourishing of humans, then taking time to consider how we relate to non-human animals is important. The Christian organization *Creature Kind* aims to resource churches to think carefully about this in practical terms.[34] It does not aim principally to make converts to vegetarianism, but encourages Christians to attend to the ethics of consumption and their participation in the economy of meat production. It provides educational resources for individuals, churches and small groups wanting to think theologically about non-human animals, as well as advice about how to source food from places where the flourishing of the fellow creature has been taken seriously.

One particularly helpful resource is the 'Friendly Food Challenge' toolkit. The toolkit was developed from a series of student and faculty-led events at Providence University College, Canada, and has been described by its founder, Michael Gilmour, as 'throwing rocks at giants' in its scale and impact. Its significance has been as a protest and a prophetic sign of what will be.[35] Once per week, on Wednesday lunchtimes, some students on the university campus have opted for a plant-based meal instead of meat products, advertised the fact, and then invited others to come and do the same. The project is about 'friendliness' because it concerns the interspecies mutuality and fellowship that the doctrine of creation entails. As momentum has grown, the weekly event has developed to include education on animal welfare, meat production, and environmental issues relating directly to food as well as human health, diet and wellbeing. Gilmour reports limited and relatively small numbers of students taking up the challenge,[36] but notes its potential for the future. Its importance in our consideration is not its size or impact, but its consistency with a Christian vision of the relationship between human and non-human animals. Gilmour's model is about instantiating Christian beliefs in the immediacy of choices around diet and menu on a weekly basis; if non-human animals have a distinct *telos* that is not fully enacted in their consumption as a human food-source, then the decisions Christians make in a cafeteria queue matter. This is the sort of challenge that may be inferred for congregations, youth groups, and church councils, as well as individual worshippers. A similar movement with origins in UK is *#defaultveg* which encourages businesses, companies, organizations, churches, schools, hospitals and community groups to 'offer plant-based meals by default, and give diners the choice to add animals products to their meals optionally'.[37] Organizations can sign up to receive help creating a tailored menu that meets the dietary needs of a group without compromising on the ethical issues associated with meat production. Default Veg lists three benefits of such a strategy:

> Reducing greenhouse gasses and emissions, associated mainly with cattle farming, and thus having a positive impact on global warming and climate change.[38]
> Reducing health risks associated with over consumption of meat.[39]
> Contributing to animal welfare and reduction of intensive meat production.

The third is most relevant to our discussion here, but it is helpful to note the wider implications of the choices involved for the general good of the environment and future generations.[40] Such additional benefits extend and add weight to the theological concerns about non-human animals and their flourishing. If meat production reduces the overall flourishing of creation, and consumption has a negative impact on human health too, then it makes sense for Christians to reject a meat-based diet in favour of a plant-based one.

The doctrine of creation reminds Christians of our connection to non-human animals and the significance of our mutual relationship as recipients of God's grace. This grace in creation also determines our interaction with fellow creatures and regulates our behaviour towards them. What does not serve their flourishing should be rejected as illegitimate Christian discipleship.

## Questions

What do you think of the idea that God creates all creatures, including non-human animals, with their own distinct meaning and purpose?

What difference could it make to your consumption of non-human animals to remember the doctrine creation when you plan meals?

## Further Reading

Clough, David, *On Animals*, Vol. 1: *Systematic Theology* (London: Bloomsbury, 2011); and *On Animals*, Vol. 2: *Theological Ethics* (London: Bloomsbury, 2019).

McFarland, Ian A., *From Nothing: A Theology of Creation* (Louisville: Westminster John Knox, 2014).

### Notes

1 See Richard Dawkins, *The Blind Watchmaker* (London: Penguin Books, 1986); and also his *The God Delusion* (New York: Bantam Books, 2006); Sam Harris, *The End of Faith: Religion, Terror, and the Future of Reason* (New York: W.W. Norton, 2004); Christopher Hitchens, *God is Not Great: The Case Against Religion* (London: Atlantic Books, 2007).

2  See Alister McGrath, *The Twilight of Atheism* (London: Doubleday, 2004); and also his *The Dawkins Delusion* (London: SPCK, 2007).

3  See the opinion-piece by Jeff Sparrow, 'We Can Save Atheism from New Atheists like Richard Dawkins and Sam Harris', *The Guardian*, 29 November 2015,www.theguardian.com/commentisfree/2015/nov/30/we-can-save-atheism-from-the-new-atheists (accessed January 2019).

4  For more on this see Karl Barth, 'God the Creator', in *Dogmatics in Outline* (London: SCM, 1949), ch. 8; and Colin Gunton, 'The Doctrine of Creation', in Gunton (ed.), *The Cambridge Companion to Christian Doctrine* (Cambridge: Cambridge University Press, 1997), 141–57.

5  For more on the complexity see, for example, John Rogerson, *Genesis 1–11* (London: T&T Clark International, 2004); or David L. Peterson, 'The Formation of the Pentateuch', in James Luther Mays et al. (eds), *Old Testament Interpretation: Past, Present, and Future* (Edinburgh: T&T Clark, 1995), 31–45.

6  Gordon J. Wenham, *Genesis 1–15*, Word Biblical Commentary Series (Nashville: Thomas Nelson, 1987), 12–13, 16.

7  Gunton, 'The Doctrine of Creation', 147.

8 Gerhard von Rad, *Genesis*, Old Testament Library (London: SCM Press, 1972), 51.

9  Neil B. MacDonald, *Metaphysics and the God of Israel: Systematic Theology of the Old and New Testaments* (Grand Rapids: Baker Academic, 2006), 46.

10  On the link between Ephesians 1 and Genesis 1, see Walter Brueggemann, *Genesis* (Louisville: Westminster John Knox, 2010), 17–21.

11 Karl Barth, *Dogmatics in Outline* (London: SCM Press, 1949), 50.

12  Kathryn Tanner, *Christ the Key* (Cambridge: Cambridge University Press, 2009); Rowan Williams, *Christ: the Heart of Creation* (London: Bloomsbury Continuum, 2018).

13 See also, MacDonald, *Metaphysics and the God of Israel*, 46–8.

14  Donald Wood, 'Maker of Heaven and Earth', *International Journal of Systematic Theology* Vol. 14.4 (2012), 385.

15  Paul van Buren, *The Austin Dogmatics*, ed. Ellen Charry (Eugene, OR: Cascade, 2012), 144.

16  Ian A. McFarland, *From Nothing: A Theology of Creation* (Louisville: Westminster John Knox Press, 2014), 21. Though the Old Testament scholar Walter Eichrodt argued that 'the ultimate aim of the narrative is the same as our formula creation *ex nihilo*', which is to present God as the originator of everything that is. See his *Theology of the Old Testament*, Vol. 2 (Philadelphia: Westminster Press, 1967), 101–2.

17 From his letter *To Autolycus*, quoted in McFarland, *From Nothing*, 2.

18  Gunton, 'The Doctrine of Creation', 141.

19 For example, other second-century bishops such as Irenaeus certainly agreed in his *Against Heretics* 3.10, and later Augustine wrote of God that, 'You did not work as a human craftsman does, making one thing out of something else', in his *Confessions*, 11.5.7. As a confessional statement see, for example,

the fourth clause of the The Westminster Confession of Faith (1646) where it is explicit, 'It pleased God ... to create or make of nothing the world ...'

20 Neil Messer, 'Humans, Animals, Evolution and Ends', in *Respecting Life: Theology and Bioethics* (London: SCM, 2011), 177.

21 Clough's two-volume work on the theology and ethics of animals is the most significant work to be published on the topic: David Clough, *On Animals, Vol. 1: Systematic Theology* (London: Bloomsbury, 2011) and *On Animals, Vol. 2: Theological Ethics* (London: Bloomsbury, 2019).

22 David Clough, *On Animals, Vol. 1*, 27.

23 David Clough, 'Consuming Animal Creatures: The Christian Ethics of Eating Animals', *Studies in Christian Ethics*, Vol. 30.1 (2017), 37.

24 Clough, 'Consuming Animal Creatures', 31.

25 Hannah Ritchie, 'Which Countries Eat the Most Meat?' www.bbc.co.uk/news/health-47057341 (accessed February 2019).

26 Compassion in World Farming, *The Life of Broiler Chickens*, www.ciwf.org.uk/media/5235306/The-life-of-Broiler-chickens.pdf (accessed January 2019).

27 See Compassion in World Farming's website, www.ciwf.org.uk/farm-animals/chickens/meat-chickens/#growth (accessed February 2019).

28 www.rspcaassured.org.uk/farm-animal-welfare/pigs.

29 Lizzie Rivera, 'The Truth Behind the Pork We Eat', *The Independent,* 29 June 2017.

30 www.rspcaassured.org.uk/farm-animal-welfare/pigs.

31 Clough, 'Consuming Animal Creatures', 40.

32 Heather Saul, 'Hatched, Discarded, Gassed: What Happens to Male Chicks in the UK', *The Independent*, 5 March 2015, www.independent.co.uk/life-style/food-and-drink/hatched-discarded-gassed-what-happens-to-male-chicks-in-the-uk-10088509.html (accessed January 2019).

33 Clough, *On Animals*, Vol. 1, 156.

34 For more information see www.becreaturekind.org.

35 www.becreaturekind.org/blog-posts/2018/2/14/throwing-rocks-at-giants (accessed March 2019).

36 Over a three-month period, with an average of 340 lunches served on campus on Wednesdays, only 250 Friendly Food choices were made. Assuming three months is about 12 weeks, then roughly 6% of the meals served were plant-based, www.becreaturekind.org/blog-posts/2018/2/14/throwing-rocks-at-giants.

37 See https://defaultveg.com.

38 One recent study has argued that this is the single biggest reason for amending food consumption to include more plant-based diets: Marco Springmann et al., 'Options for Keeping the Food System within Environmental Limits', *Nature: International Journal of Science,* Vol. 562 (2018), 519–26. See also, Sarah Gibbens, 'Eating Meat has Dire Consequences for the Planet, Says Report', *National Geographic*, 16 January 2019, www.nationalgeographic.com/environment/2019/01/commission-report-great-food-transformation-plant-diet-climate-change/ (accessed February 2019).

39 See Louise Aston, James Smith, and John Powles, 'Impacts of a Reduced Red and Processed Meat Dietary Pattern on Disease Risks and Greenhouse Gas Emissions in the UK: A Modelling Story', *BMJ Open,* Vol. 2.5 (2012), https://bmjopen.bmj.com/content/bmjopen/2/5/e001072.full.pdf (accessed March 2019).

40 See also, Hanna Tuomisto, 'Importance of Considering Environmental Sustainability in Dietary Guidlines', *The Lancet: Planetary Health Open* Vol.2.8(2018),www.thelancet.com/journals/lanplh/article/PIIS2542-5196%2818%2930174-8/fulltext (accessed March 2019).

# 4

# 'In One Lord, Jesus Christ': Political Responsibility

In 1988, the then Archbishop of Cape Town, Desmund Tutu, was involved in the undoing of the apartheid regime in South Africa. It brought him into conflict with a variety of people, including the national President, P. W. Botha. Himself a professed Christian, Botha wanted Tutu to keep out of politics. He regarded the Archbishop's interference as a distortion of the gospel and an abuse of his position within the nation's life. Tutu responded in a lengthy letter, outlining from Scripture exactly why participation in political discourse was a necessary Christian activity. It culminated with a now infamous challenge: 'The God whom we worship is the Lord of all life, and if we are to say his writ does not run in the political realm then you need to tell us whose writ does?'[1] Tutu's justification for the perceived infringement on politics was God's lordly concern for all of creation. And as a disciple of this God, Tutu was also obliged to care and to demonstrate that he cared by speaking up and getting involved. Precisely because Christians worship the 'Lord of all life' they have a responsibility to be concerned for all spheres of life, and this is no less true in the complex and sometimes competing relationship of politics and religion. In the Nicene Creed, Christ's lordship is central to a web of personal and corporate relationships in which he is one who has power and authority over all creation, who lovingly lays claim to it, and who commands something of human agents. 'Jesus is my Lord' is a statement of allegiance made by those who follow him; 'Jesus is our Lord' is the corporate acknowledgement and worship of Christ's Church; but, in the Christian tradition, 'Jesus is the Lord' is a statement that pertains to creation as a whole, whether

Christ's position and power and authority is recognized and owned by the human beings within it or not. That was Tutu's motivation, and it is the theme of this chapter.

## The Earliest Confession of Faith

'Jesus Christ is Lord' is the major claim of the New Testament (Rom. 10.9; 1 Cor. 12.3; Phil. 2.11). That it is the most ancient of the Church's proclamations, pre-dating the composition of the individual elements of the scriptural canon by some years, is evidenced by the presence of the Aramaic formula, *marana tha* (1 Cor. 16.22) a compound phrase that can mean either 'Come, O Lord!' or 'Our Lord has come!' (cf. Rev. 22.20). In both instances the 'Lord' who is named is Jesus Christ. The phrase has clearly survived intact as a loanword from the earliest Jewish-Christian congregations and is transliterated into the Greek of the New Testament. This suggests it is a phrase that would have been recognized in and of itself by the increasingly diverse and non-Aramaic Christian communities that had arisen by the mid-first century. In a similar way words and phrases like 'Amen' and 'Alleluia' have remained from Hebrew into Greek and now English because their regular and specialized liturgical use warranted their transliteration rather than translation. According to biblical scholars, precisely what may be meant by Jesus' lordship is layered with possibility. It has both religious and political meanings, and political and ethical implications.

The word 'lord' translates the Greek *kyrios*, and the Hebrew *mari*, and in its basic form could refer to 'any person possessing power and authority'.[2] In popular Greek culture it was used within the master-slave relationship meaning something similar to 'sir', while it was used within the cultic environment of Hellensitic paganism to express respect for the gods by calling them 'lord'.[3] In the Bible it is used in the Septuagint translation of the Old Testament with the definite article to denote God's name revealed in the tetragrammaton (YHWH), and without the definite article to refer to another person of power. This is the case, for example, in Psalm 110.1, 'The LORD [o kyrios/ YHWH] said to my lord [kyroi mou/adonai] sit at my right hand.' By the time the so-called 'Christ hymns' were composed and in use in the early Church it is clear that references to lordship were a significant part of Jewish-Christian praise and worship of Jesus. St Paul quoted from such compositions, and the Johannine prologue (John 1.1–14) is sometimes thought to be another example. They're especially useful for helping us to explore the meaning of Christ's lordship.

## The Philippians' Christ Hymn

Probably the most famous and most recognizable of the New Testament Christ hymns is Philippians 2.6–11:

> ... who, though he was in the form of God,
> did not regard equality with God as something to be exploited,
> but emptied himself, taking the form of a slave, being born in human likeness.
> And being found in human form, he humbled himself
> and became obedient to the point of death– even death on a cross.
>
> Therefore God also highly exalted him and gave him the name
> that is above every name, so that at the name of Jesus every knee should bend,
> in heaven and on earth and under the earth, and every tongue should confess
> that Jesus Christ is Lord, to the glory of God the Father.

This is a hymn about Christ rather than to him (cf. Eph. 5.19), but none the less it celebrates that Jesus Christ is Lord in two ways.[4] First, it looks back to and narrates the work of Christ with reference to key biographical moments: the incarnation, suffering and humiliation, subsequent death as a criminal, and then final exaltation. It makes clear overtures to the eternal history of the Son (though, interestingly, Paul says this of Jesus Christ in v. 5, not restricting his comments about eternality to the pre-incarnate Son/Word) as one who both shared the *form* of God and thus also *equality* with God. This eternal status was then compromised by taking on the *form* of a human slave and thus, we may infer, by taking on equality with humanity.[5] The shock and humiliation of weakness is celebrated in this hymn rather than sublimated, which indicates something of the kind of lordship Christ exercises: humble, self-emptying and salvific. The point is extended if the end of the first stanza[6] and the beginning of the second are not juxtaposed, but understood as a natural development within God's economy; the 'therefore' implies that the humiliation and death of Christ were necessary and the Father's approval of the fact may be inferred from his exaltation of Christ. The exaltation is, no doubt, a euphemism for the resurrection and ascension. It's unlikely that the hymn writer thought of these simply in terms of a return to a former state of equality with God. The Greek term implies a kind of 'hyper exaltation' and the subsequent turn towards the cosmic significance for every person and every creature (rather than the religious community of the Church) is probably what is meant. The very particular person, Jesus Christ, has become the universal Lord. The one who was a slave is now worshipped with God. Christ's resurrection life is all encompassing.

With the turn to exaltation the principal subject of the hymn changes. We move from Christ emptying and humbling himself to God the Father exalting him. The passivity of Christ here is perhaps meant to demonstrate that he really was dead. Dead people can't do much for themselves. It reflects the passivity found in other New Testament texts where the resurrection is described as something that happened *to* Christ rather than that which he did for himself, as a vindication perhaps of his humility and obedience (Acts 2.24; Acts 13.30; Rom. 10.9; Eph. 1.20). His actions are further vindicated with the conferral of a significant name. Given the likelihood that this hymn originated in a Jewish-Christian context, we might suppose that this name is God's own name being shared with Jesus since the section is based upon a parallel verse in Isaiah 45.23, 'to me every knee shall bow and every tongue swear'. We learn from the preceding verse in Isaiah that the subject of the passage is God who has come to offer help and salvation to 'all the ends of the earth'. This Christ hymn follows the same theme of salvation, but here links it directly to Jesus Christ who is also, therefore, the one before whom every knee should bow and every tongue confess. Some scholars have argued that the final crescendo of worship – 'to the glory of God the Father' – indicates that this Christ hymn was part of a bigger eucharistic liturgy in which the story of salvation was retold[7] and the work of God in and for creation was celebrated. Others have placed it within the existing Judaic hymnic tradition which continued within the early Jewish-Christian congregation. If this is the case, it adds further weight to the close connection between God and Christ suggested in the poetry, since only God was praised in hymnic fashion in the Jewish tradition.[8] Either way, that we're considering an early first-century hymn is a significant theological point in and of itself: the Lord Jesus Christ has been worshipped and glorified from the earliest days of the Church in a way in which no other person of significance within the Jewish tradition had been before or since.

The second way the hymn celebrates Christ's lordship is by shifting the focus of our thoughts from the past to the present to the future. The movement is important because it maps out for us the shape of the Christocentric metaphysics at work in St Paul's understanding of the Christian life: Christ was dead, but now he is alive and has ascended to the place of honour and worship, and will one day receive the worship and adoration of all creation at the eschaton. When Christians say 'Jesus is Lord' all three of these aspects are in view: he is Lord because of his death; he is Lord because of the resurrection and ascension; he is Lord because he will one day be worshipped as such by everybody. And all three of these aspects have radical implications for those who believe them. His death was *for* sinful creatures; his resurrection enables those same creatures to live freely from the power of sin and death; the eschaton is the goal to which all of creation is heading. Like all creatures, Christians remain caught up in this meta-narrative. They confess Jesus' lordship in the present, but do so proleptically anticipating his universal lordship in the future. St Paul articulated something of the tension when he wrote elsewhere, 'creation waits with eager longing for the revealing of the children of God ... in hope that creation itself will be set free from its bondage to decay and obtain the freedom of the glory of the children of God' (Rom. 8.19–21). Christians wait and long for the fulfilment of what they confess to be true now and will be true in the future when they affirm 'Jesus is Lord', but do so *actively* as those who must live as Christ's disciples in the in-between time.

## The Scope of Lordship

'Jesus is Lord' is an all-encompassing claim. Tutu remembered what Botha did not: that calling Jesus 'Lord' has never been a matter of simple respect or personal piety. He is not to be confused with other cultic figures in the wider world. As St Paul wrote elsewhere of the pagan shrines, '... even though there may be many so-called gods under heaven or on earth, yet for us there is one God ... and one Lord, Jesus Christ ...' (1 Cor. 8.5–6). Christianity admits no competitors alongside Christ. Moreover, Christ's lordship requires something from us, 'as Christians, our personal obedience is claimed and all institutions are set under Christ's authority'.[9] Such an approach to religion was unusual in the pre-Constantinian Roman Empire, where pluralism and syncretism was common. Exclusive devotion could be offensive to the state's religion, and to the Caesar who was worshipped as a god. The Roman Empire required allegiance because the stability of the state was its highest good; competing metanarratives were suspected of treason, wanting to destabilize the citizenry. They were very often opposed and rejected. But confessing Christ as Lord could not be simply a matter of personal piety, as if Jesus should be more accurately described as 'lord of the Church' or 'lord of the Christian people' and that only when it doesn't conflict with other commitments to the state etc. On the contrary, the force and extent of the claim of Christ's lordship has always been interpreted with both particular and universal scope: he is my Lord (John 20.28) and he is Lord of all (1 Cor. 8.6). The Nicene Council codified a belief that they knew already had significant political ramifications beyond the Church. Christ's relevance is cosmic, and his sovereignty absolute. He is the one before whom every knee will bow and every tongue confess (Phil. 2.11), and who will have the first place in everything (Col. 1.18). He is the one through whom all things were made (John 1.3), and therefore the one to lay claim to all created things under God. Christ is the one whom the whole world will one day acknowledge as King of Kings and Lord of Lords (Rev. 17.14; 19.16). More than simple devotion and admiration, the Church's proclamation of Christ's lordship has always meant something good for the world too.

*****

Believing in Christ's universal lordship leads to the Church's commitment to the world for which Christ died, has been raised, and over which he will one day reign. That is to say that the Christian community's Christocentric exclusivism is not an excuse to withdraw from society; rather it is the impetus for the Church's work and witness within the world for the good of the world. Jesus instructs his disciples to be 'salt and light' for the good of the world, rather than simply for the good of the Church (Matt. 5.13–16). This good is both spiritual, in making disciples of all nations (Matt. 28.19), and also practical, in treating others as neighbours who are worthy recipients of love and care. But, as Tutu suggested to Botha, in emphasizing the lordship of Christ this clause of the Creed invites us to participate in especially political terms. Politics is about the ordering of society and the regulation of power. It is about what is most valuable to that society, and the ways in which those values play out in common life.

## Latent Participation

There is a general sense in which the Church participates in the political life of a nation as a particular constituent of civil society. Substantial accounts of the spiritual and religious capital that the Church has to offer have been drawn up in recent years.[10] Much of this is cultural and historical, such as buildings and architecture, but a lot of it is sociological and attitudinal.[11] The latter is more difficult to quantify but is generally regarded as much more important for a healthy society: religious organizations are community groups and often community organizers, providing voluntary services and committing to localities long after Council-run services have been removed, but most importantly being present with and within communities, building meaningful relationships and enabling social cohesion.[12] The rapid rise of Food Banks in the midst of social and economic crisis leaving 14m people living in poverty in the UK (of which 6.5m are children) is one indication of the resources available to Church groups working in local communities.[13] Such positivity sits alongside growing tensions about religion in public life: the rise of religious extremism on the one hand and globalism on the other means that the place of religion is society is confused and complicated.[14] The Church's general participation is an accidental hangover of the historical influence of Christianity; it is also a result of the establishment of the Church of England.

## Towards the Common Good

The more particular way in which Christians have thought about political involvement is first to do with the vision for which they work, what is often called *the common good*. In contrast to ideas of commonality that depend on weight of numbers, where the greatest good is what serves the greatest number of people, the Christian understanding of the term relates to the question of the ultimate meaning or purpose of society, what constitutes the good health and fulfilment of its members, and what political structures and processes are necessary to achieve those ends. It usually involves concern for the shared and mutual benefits of belonging to society, and the assumption that both institutions and private citizens work best when they work together to fulfil those concerns.[15] Christianity's commitment to the common good is its commitment to the welfare of its neighbours under God. It is informed by a vision for society that grows out of the theological anthropology of the gospel. That means that Christian ideas of the common good are rooted in God's creative intention for human beings revealed in Jesus Christ. John Chrysostom said that working towards the common good 'is the rule of most perfect Christianity, its most exact definition, its highest point ... for nothing can so make a person an imitator of Christ as caring for his neighbours'.[16] Several times Jesus gave instruction that love of neighbour was central to the common good (Matt. 22.36–40; Mark 12.30–31), and furthermore redefined who neighbours were by transforming the bonds between people. In the Kingdom of God, the former bonds of peace – race, ethnicity and filial connections – no longer took precedence over the common bond of humanity (Luke 10.25–37; cf. Gal. 3.28). Jesus challenged the social structures of his day by calling those who followed him not simply to care for and feast with those who had the wealth and status to repay, but to share with the poor on the highways and byways, whose position meant no chance of reciprocity (Luke 14.12–14). He accorded women a dignity for which the rest of society was unprepared (John 4.5–42; Mark 5.25–34). Neighbours provide an opportunity to love another, and therefore to grow into the kind of people that Christ calls Christians to become. This is meant to be liberating rather than limiting, as we are set free to fulfil the purpose for which we were created.[17] Furthermore, Jesus' earliest preaching pointed people toward the coming Kingdom in which the weakest in society – the poor, the sick, the excluded – would find healing, satisfaction and liberation (Luke 4.18). Christians believe in the common good because, through baptism, they live Christ's life and share Christ's concern for the world (Rom. 6.3–11).

## Affirmation and Challenge

Precisely because Christians are concerned with the kind of common good that matters to Jesus Christ, political participation means both affirmation and challenge of civil structures. This point is developed in various ways throughout the New Testament. Christians are instructed to be a blessing to society, to live in peace with everyone (Rom. 12.18) and submit to the ruling authorities (Rom. 13.1) including the emperor (1 Pet. 2.13), remembering that all authority comes from God (cf. John 19.11). Christians are told to pay their taxes whether they agree with the authorities or not (Matt. 22.21; Mark 12.17; cf. Luke 23.2) and pray for those who exercise political power (1 Tim. 2.2). Christians should not fear addressing those in power (Acts 24.10–22) because the real authority belongs to Christ (Matt. 28.18; 1 Pet. 3.22). The earliest Christians modelled a different sort of economic practice, holding wealth and possessions in common (Acts 2.42–7; 4.32–7) for the good of the whole community (2 Cor. 9.1–8). And these specifically named practices in the New Testament should be set alongside the Old Testament principles of justice and fairness (Deut. 21.10–14; 19.15), care for the marginalized poor – especially the orphans and widows (Ps. 72.2–4), proper care and regard for foreigners (Lev. 24.22), generosity towards enemies (Prov. 25.21), helpful economic policies (Lev. 25.1–10), and the rule of law with which the earliest Christians would have been very familiar. The point of these principles and practices was to live well before God in a world that might not regard or worship God, but which is, none the less, the focus of God's beneficent activity (Matt. 5.45). Where there is cross-over between God's purpose and vision for human beings then that is to be celebrated and affirmed. In our contemporary context that may mean support for public welfare policy as an example of care and active regard for the poorest in society; or championing fair immigration laws as an example of proper regard for foreigners. Christians need not persistently agitate against the state, but can and must support and bless the state that does God's will.

But there are times when it may be necessary to challenge as well as affirm. Christians can never take civil society fully seriously as a project in and of itself because they are a people who are ultimately subjects of a different authority (Acts 17.7) but who participate at that authority's pleasure. Followers of Jesus are resident aliens: 'our citizenship is in heaven, and it is from there that we are expecting a saviour, the Lord Jesus Christ' (Phil. 3.20; cf. 1 Pet. 2.11–17). The sign and seal of this citizenship is baptism, through which people die to themselves and are resurrected with Christ for the purposes of God (Rom. 6.6–11). By this sacramental act Christians refuse absolute loyalty to the state, pledging instead their absolute devotion to Christ. But in so doing they pledge themselves to the *cause* of Christ, and this means the health and wholeness of human society. Christians are servants of a different master, but one who has committed himself to seeking and enabling God's good purpose for humanity.

Baptismal citizenship is, therefore, not permission for Christians to be irritating or difficult within civil society; neither is it a mandate for protest. It is, rather, a reminder that a Christian community that is faithful to Christ will sometimes find that it cannot be 'accommodated to existing political societies … assuring existing authorities that they will not be disturbed by it'.[18] Participation in civil society does not equal sublimation of the society of the baptized. This is precisely because the Church's vision for a common good is discernable only from within the re-ordered metaphysics of the gospel. Thus, theologically speaking, the common good is not what society says is good for itself, but what the gospel says is good for society. Of course, it should not be assumed that the Church knows God's mind without help, and that its contribution to the vision of the common good is its own rather than something that it discerns. Neither should it be assumed that the Church desires theocracy this side of the eschaton. The Christian community must think and reflect and pray in order to understand God's intention for society, perceiving through the lens of faith, in much the same way that 'the ascended Christ who governs [the Church] is to be discerned by faith'.[19] This is what lay behind Tutu's letter to Botha in 1988. Christians must remain free as they participate by remaining orientated towards Christ the Lord; free as disciples to follow him. Their freedom may be exercised as their vocation requires to agitate and provoke civil society towards a better service of the common good; to speak prophetically into difficult and complex situations; to risk the ire of those in power. Any attempt to acquiesce or opt out is a denial of the baptismal vocation to serve Christ in the world.

## Democracy and Power

Participation is not abstraction but contextualization. The Church plays its part within a particular space and time, culture and history. In western Christianity the political context is essentially democratic, the great gift of which is the ability to put limitations on the exercise of power.[20] Limiting and directing the use of power to prevent its abuses have been important considerations in the West since the Enlightenment's rejection of absolute binding authorities. Democracy means 'the people's judgement'. In most democratic nation states, the judgement of the people is exercised by vote. In a liberal indirect democracy (i.e. where those elected are representatives rather than delegates) such as that in the UK, the rights and freedoms of the people are protected, and the processes of election are governed by law to formalize proper checks and balances. But the idea of democracy involves much more than mechanisms of power-management.

The ethos of democracy is shared responsibility and access to power for all. It grows out of a general scepticism and suspicion that any one constituent member of society will necessarily exercise power to the good of all members, and so democratic ideologies aim at justice and fairness by prohibiting monopolization.[21] As Reinhold Niebuhr expressed it, 'Man's capacity for justice makes democracy possible; but man's inclination for injustice makes democracy necessary.'[22] The vision is for mutual flourishing through corporate responsibility and ownership, the sharing out of power, and the prevention of injustice by providing structural checks and balances.[23] In recent years there has been a crisis in democracy in the West, driven by a sense of disaffection among the young and a general disenchantment with politics evidenced in lower voter turnouts, growing dissatisfaction from political parties, and an increasing sense of disconnection from the political classes with the rise of the so-called professional political class (i.e. an MP who hasn't ever had another job).[24] In this context, other kinds of democratic participation have gained more traction. Protest groups are blossoming, as are marches and public demonstrations, community organizers and localized issues groups. Constituencies want their voices to be heard, and will find ways of doing it. It is important to note, therefore, that while democratic processes diversify, the key idea remains the same: to safeguard against monopolization of power, and thus to prevent injustice, by opening up the political sphere to competing voices. Put more positively, its aim is for the health and wellbeing of all in society by the appropriate use of power to the benefit of all.

In many ways democracy can seem antithetical to Christianity.

'Jesus Christ is Lord', and thus nobody else is, including the majority voting public. This same Lord is also judge, and justice is, therefore, the fulfilment of God's will. But, as we saw in Philippians 2, when Christians proclaim the authority of Christ they do so proleptically – believing it to be true now while anticipating its civil fulfilment at the eschaton, 'when every knee shall bow and every tongue confess'. Christians await that day with joy, but we must also inhabit our own day until it comes. Democracy is a concession to the brokenness of the world in our in-between state: democratic processes are to be supported as the best means of preventing the abuse of power as we await Christ's coming in glory.[25] In the end, Christians believe in benevolent sovereign authority. But it is not yet the end. Therefore, democracy provides useful points of access for Christians to share in the constructive work of building society for the common good. It makes it possible for the Christian voice to be used and for it to be heard. And the tone of this voice matters: Christians must engage in persuasion and argumentation, rather than direct proselytizing or judgemental condescension. To that extent, participation in liberal democracy requires wisdom. All this is not to say liberal democracy is perfect. Any advocacy of Christian political participation is not geared towards defending democracy in and of itself, but towards maximizing the possibilities that democracy affords a Christian vision of the common good.

## The Practicalities of Participation

What, then, are the means of participation for Christians sojourning in a western democracy, and who are seeking the common good within society? Participation does not mean affirmation or even absolute integration. It does mean something more basic, 'playing our part'. This, I suggest, is both our part as particular citizens within civil society, ensuring that that the democratic impulse to prevent a monopoly on power is upheld and defended, and the part that has been given to the Church by God within the economy of grace to be salt and light in the world. I am most concerned in this closing section with the implications for individual Christians. What should we do? What does the Lordship of Christ imply for the part we might play?

The obvious suggestion is that eligible Christians should use their vote in all types of elections as a positive influence towards the common good. Sometimes Christians have argued that active participation in politics is not necessary for the Church because God is in control and all will work out well in the end. But this claim suggests that what happens now is not as important as what will come in the future. It juxtaposes the sacred and secular. It runs contrary to the argument about the Lordship of Christ requiring our constructive engagement in the world for which Christ died and now lives. It also disregards the Church's call to be salt and light, and to make a positive difference to the world as we await Christ's coming. It simply will not do; Christians must vote. But how Christians vote will always be tricky, and a matter of conscience; no single political party or single politician will embody entirely the views and values of their voters, even if the politician is a Christian. If Christians take the call to participate seriously, then voting requires thought: 'Christians must examine the rival party-programmes on offer and reach their best judgement of which to support ...'[26] This means distinguishing between defining issues for the society at large, and single issues about which individual Christians or whole denominations might care, but which might be relativized at the ballot box by concerns for the common good. 'While single issues ... have limited impact on other areas of policy, defining issues ... have systemic impact on many other areas.'[27] What then follows is a decision about casting votes positively, in favour of a particular candidate, or negatively, to block out the worst candidate. My concern here is for the drivers that shape our voting: concern for the welfare of the whole community. Christians do not need to show their concern for the common good publicly; what happens in the privacy of the ballot box is just as important before God.

Aside from voting, there are other means of participation. The para-Church organization, *Christians in Politics,* has developed a helpful matrix for thinking about politics in a range of ways.[28] The aim is to give structure to our thinking and to encourage Christians to take the Lordship of Christ seriously by being present within political structures to exercise some influence for the common good. The matrix consists of two principal axes: the first locates the level of participation, whether local politics or national politics, and the second denotes the type of participation, whether issue-based campaigning, party politics or public service.[29] Each of the types is then described across the matrix. So, one way to engage in campaigning at a local level is to write to your MP on a topic that is important to your region or neighbourhood, or to lobby your local councillors for change. At a national level, Christians might join a campaigning organization or join marches and demonstrations, organize petitions or go door-to-door canvasing opinions and sharing information. This issue-based approach has a long history within the Church: it was done by William Wilberforce on slavery and Martin Luther-King on segregation. It motivated both the populace and the government. With regard to public service at a local level, Christians might volunteer to be school governors or join the police force or staff homeless shelters. They can join community action groups, neighbourhood watch, or become a local magistrate. At a national level they may work in the civil service or organizations such as the NHS or military. Some Christians use their skills as researchers or communicators to work for think-tanks; others might use their influence in business or industry to contribute to national debates and discourse. A small number of Christians might join political parties and stand for elections in local and national seats. The idea in each of these circumstances is to discern the best means of participation to seek the common good under Christ's Lordship.

## Summary

The Church does seek to replace existing forms of civil government with theocracy. It must live under the lordship of Christ by undoing the separation of the world and Church, and seeing itself as called to the world for Christ's sake. As Tutu knew, Christ is not only lord of the Church nor is civil society a godless place. Church is a mediating force for Christ, as the political society in which Jesus' lordship is recognized and valued. Christian citizenship is imbalanced dual-citizenship (i.e. more Churchly than civil) precisely because it is caught up in a partially realized state; Jesus Christ is (the Church's) Lord, and Jesus Christ will be (the world's) Lord. It requires prayerful discernment, 'because we're not praying so that God can do our will but so that we can understand what God's will is'.[30] Discernment means living in the world for which Christ died as if he really is alive, despite the fact the world in which we live does not recognize him, precisely because we believe it will be to the world's own good, and because one day it will be so. To confess that Jesus Christ is Lord is to tell the truth about all that is, and to recognize the ways in which his Lordship is yet to be fully realized. It is to be caught between the present and the future. Christ is Lord because God exalted him by raising him from the dead; Christ will be Lord when he comes again in glory. The Church's task is to inhabit that tension, knowing both to be true.

## Questions

How often do you pray about your vote in a local or national election?

Do you think faith has any role in our political choices? Why?

In what ways could you put your faith into practice by actively pursuing the common good in your local community?

# Further Reading

Cuff, Simon, *Love in Action: Catholic Social Teaching for Every Church* (London: SCM Press, 2019).

Williams, Rowan, *Faith in the Public Square* (London: Bloomsbury, 2012).

## Notes

1 Cited in Peter Steinfels, 'Tutu and Botha Joust Over Theology', *The New York Times*, 3 May 1988.

2 I. Howard Marshall, *The Origins of New Testament Christology* (Leicester: Inter-Varsity Press, 1976), 97.

3 Marshall, *Origins*, 104.

4 For more on the patterns associated with hymnic artistry see Michael Wade Martin and Bryan Nash, 'Philippians 2.6–11 as Subversive *Hymnos*: A Study in the Light of Ancient Rhetorical Theory' in *The Journal of Theological Studies* Vol. 66.1 (2015), 90–138.

5 There is some debate among New Testament scholars about the meaning of 'exploited' v. 6b. *Harpagmos* can suggest several options, and so the question is 'does it mean that Christ enjoyed equality with God but surrendered it by becoming man, or that he could have grasped at equality with God by self-assertion but declined to do so?' See Ralph Martin, *Philippians: An Introduction and Commentary* (Nottingham: Inter-Varsity Press Academic, 2008), 97. Martin's alternative suggestion is that the verse celebrates the Son's humility by denoting the Son's willingness to obey the Father by refusing to exploit his eternal position within the Godhead, and thus to enable the salvation of humankind.

6 In using the idea of stanzas I am following the suggestion of Graham Stanton among others, who sees v. 9 as denoting a shift in thinking within the hymn. See his *Jesus of Nazareth in New Testament Preaching* (Cambridge: Cambridge University Press, 1974), 99–102.

7 See Ernst Lohmeyer, *Der Brief an Philipper* (Göttingen: Vandenhoeck and Ruprecht, 1956).

8 Larry Hurtado, *One God, One Lord: Early Christian Devotion and Ancient Jewish Monotheism* (Edinburgh: T&T Clark, 1998), 102–4.

9 John Ashcroft, 'The Biblical Agenda: Issues of Interpretation' in *The Jubilee Agenda: A Framework, Agenda and Strategy for Christian Social Reform* (Leicester: Inter-Varsity Press, 2005), 86.

10 See, for example, Chris Baker and Hannah Skinner, *Faith in Action: The Dynamic Connection Between Spiritual and Religious Capital* (London: William Temple Foundation, 2014), https://williamtemplefoundation. org.uk/wp-content/uploads/2014/03/Faith-In-Action-William-Temple-Foundation-2014.pdf (accessed January 2019).

11 See, for example, the list generated by Michael Turnbull and Donald McFadyen, *The State of the Church and the Church of the State: Re-imagining the Church of England for our World Today* (London: Darton, Longman & Todd, 2012), ch. 2.

12 See Bernice Martin, 'Beyond Measurement: The Non-quantifiable Religious Dimension in Social Life', in Paul Avis (ed.), *Public Faith? The State of Religious Belief and Practice in Britain* (London: SPCK, 2003), 1–18.

13 See www.trusselltrust.org/what-we-do/ (accessed December 2018). For one assessment of the value of Church-run projects see the Editorial piece, 'The Shocking Reality of Foodbanks in 2018', *The Big Issue*, 13 December 2018.

14 See Rowan Williams, *Faith in the Public Square* (London: Bloomsbury, 2012); Robert Audi and Nicholas Wolterstorff, *Religion in the Public Square: The Place of Religious Convictions in Political Debate* (London: Rowman and Littlefield, 1997).

15 The Bible Society has produced a helpful introduction to the common good in pastoral practice: *Calling People of Goodwill: The Bible and the Common Good* (London: Bible Society, 2017). Simon Cuff has also offered a summary of the catholic tradition in his *Love in Action: Catholic Social Teaching for Every Church* (London: SCM, 2019), ch. 3.

16 John Chrysostom, 'Homily 25', quoted in Jim Wallis, *The Uncommon Good: How the Gospel Brings Hope to a World Divided* (Grand Rapids: Brazos, 2014), 3.

17 On this point about freedom and love of neighbor, see Graham Tomlin, *Bound to be Free: The Paradox of Freedom* (London: Bloomsbury, 2017).

18 Oliver O'Donovan, *The Desire of the Nations: Rediscovering the Roots of Political Theology* (Cambridge: Cambridge University Press, 1996), 162.

19 O'Donovan, *Desire of the Nations*, 166.

20 On this point see Richard Harries, *Rediscovering the Christian Roots of our Political Values* (London: Darton, Longman & Todd, 2010), ch. 3.

21 Robin Gill identifies this as a particular motif of post-modern ideologies: 'it is frequently argued in a post-modern age that self-interest alone, or, perhaps more accurately, self-regarding interest alone, regulates all moral behaviour.' See his *Moral Leadership in a Postmodern Age* (Edinburgh: T&T Clark, 1997), 33.

22 Reinhold Niebuhr, *The Children of Light and the Children of Darkness: A Vindication of Democracy and a Critique of its Traditional Defenders* (London: Nisbet, 1945), vi.

23 A very helpful guide to this is Vernon Bogdanor, *The New British Constitution* (Oxford: Hart Publishing, 2009).

24 Bogdanor, *The New Constitution*, 291–3.

25 Harries, *Rediscovering*, 55–9.

26 Jonathan Chaplin, 'How Should Christians Vote in 2010?', *Ethics in Brief*, Vol. 15.2 (2010), 3.

27 Chaplin, 'How Should Christians Vote?', 3.

28 Phil Anderson, *Being Salt and Light in Politics and Government*, London: Christians in Politics, 2016, www.christiansinpolitics.org.uk/uploads/PDFs/being-salt-and-light-CiPol.pdf (accessed January 2019).

29 Anderson, *Being Salt and Light*, 9.

30 Anderson, *Being Salt and Light*, 16.

# 5

# 'Conceived of the Holy Spirit, born of the Virgin Mary': Disability and Humanity

Origins matter. Where we come from matters. It is part of our identity, and shapes our development into adulthood and beyond. It is hard to imagine anyone telling the story of Jesus without starting with the nativity; and it is hard to imagine anybody telling the story of the nativity without beginning with the annunciation. We've all sat through school nativities, or have seen the figurine versions of the holy family gathered around a cattle trough in churches. But before Mary, dressed in blue, rides the donkey to Bethlehem with Joseph out in front leading the way to the stable (very little of which is in the biblical material), she must encounter God's messenger and Joseph must have his dream. The typical play presents Mary, a young woman going about her day-to-day chores and responsibilities, interrupted and startled by Gabriel who has come to inform her that she will become pregnant. She is not to fear because this will be the work of the Holy Spirit who will 'overshadow her' so that the son whom she will bear will be God's. A little way down the gestation period, to add drama to the scene, Joseph is set to divorce her for precisely the kind of youthful infidelity that the local gossips might imagine was the real cause of her pregnancy, until the angel appears in his dream and tells him the truth. The traditional claim attached to this narrative is, therefore, threefold: that Mary was a virgin at conception; that she remained a virgin during gestation; and that she was a virgin when she was delivered of the child, Jesus. It is a rather shocking, maybe even offensive, story upon first reading. Joseph has been cuckolded by God. Mary is the incubator for the divine child. The angel doesn't ask her permission or invite her consideration. The fact that she gives a positive and consenting response is her own choice. What happens is God's will and, we may surmise, would have been fulfilled whether she had said 'yes' or 'no'. But for her willing part in it all, Mary has come to receive a significant place of honour within the history of the Church, and the virgin birth occupies a place of credal significance today.[1]

This clause of the creed is the first part of the development of the second article, 'one Lord Jesus Christ', and addresses firstly the *person* of Christ in distinction from the *work* of Christ. It is a longstanding logical rather than ontological distinction, introduced in order to give shape and structure to the field of Christology rather than because we can meaningfully discern a difference between who Jesus was/is and what Jesus did/does.[2] Indeed, the New Testament writers clearly want to help us see Jesus' true identity in and through the miraculous works he performed, his astonishing teaching, and his death and resurrection. They also want us to see who he is from the infancy narratives.

## Two Gospels, One Nativity?

An oddity of the nativity story as it is popularly told it is that it conflates two accounts, one in Matthew and the other in Luke. Each of them recounts the story slightly differently. Mark and John have no concern for the miraculous story of Jesus' conception and birth. They begin differently. But Matthew euphemistically tells us about the virgin birth, saying, 'Joseph had no marital relations with her until she had borne a son' (Matt. 1.25) and quotes Isaiah the prophet. Luke confirms what Matthew intends by making it more explicit: Mary raises the problem of her marital status and therefore virginity as a point of order for the angelic visitor, 'How can this be, since I am a virgin?' (Luke 1.34). The angel's answer was not to point to her future husband, Joseph, as the father, but to reassure her that this would be the work of the Holy Spirit. For this reason, the child 'will be called Son of God' (Luke 1.35). Thus, two of the four gospels dispense with it, and two of the four disagree over the details, though they may be made to agree over the general trajectory.

Another, more significant, oddity is that nowhere else in the New Testament is the virgin birth mentioned. In fact, the birth of Jesus is not a major concern outside of these two gospels. When St Paul gestured towards it, he was clear that Jesus was born of a woman (Gal. 4.4), but no mention of Mary's virginity or the overshadowing of the Spirit. Most likely his concern was for the incarnation-humanity of Jesus. Given that the composition of the gospels is usually reckoned to follow after that of the epistles, one would expect to find something mentioned earlier rather than only later if it was important from the beginning. The absence of the virgin birth within the early tradition is doubly conspicuous when we consider how often St Paul chose to clarify the identity and position of Jesus Christ in the New Testament epistles. A miracle of that significance would have added weight to his proclamation of Christ's divinity in Colossians, or explained exactly how God was the saviour of the world in Romans. It's odd that he didn't draw on it to make a point if he knew about it. Put positively, its absence suggests that it is possible to believe in the incarnation and the salvific work of Christ without the necessity of a virgin birth.[3] Put negatively, inconsistencies like this have been the occasion for serious critical discussion on the historical veracity and necessity of the virgin birth, and whether its function in the gospel of Matthew and the wider credal tradition was not for some other reason than historical faithfulness.

The field of study is often divided into those who affirm the credal statement without question; those who think it is historically disingenuous and should be relativized by historical-critical study; and those who think its significance is purely theological, and on that basis only should it be taken seriously.[4] To explore this further, I want to discuss three examples of theologians who fit these descriptions: Oliver Crisp, John Dominic Crossan, and Andrew Lincoln. After that, I want to suggest a way through this disagreement by orientating the discussion towards the common commitment to Christ's full humanity.

## Crisp, Crossan and Lincoln

Oliver Crisp is an analytic theologian rather than a biblical scholar.[5] His work on the virgin birth, therefore, fits within wider work on Christology, and especially the doctrine of the incarnation.[6] For Crisp, while it is possible to believe in the incarnation without the virgin birth, 'such a doctrine is still contrary to the plain teaching of Scripture and the Creeds on the question of the mode of the incarnation'.[7] The point Crisp makes is not foremost about the nature of the event, but about the identity of Jesus Christ in the light of the Chalcedonian Definition, which is the benchmark of Christian thinking on the topic. Crisp locates the virgin conception, gestation and birth alongside other Christocentric miracles of the New Testament, arguing that critics of the tradition 'cannot be opposed to the idea that God is able to perform miracles, if [they] believe that God created the world, or that God raised Christ from the dead'. Any biological problems caused by the traditional view are overshadowed by the miraculous creative activity of God – the one from whom all creaturely existence comes – such that Crisp thinks it entirely possible to believe that Mary supplied some of the DNA, and so too did the Holy Spirit (in place of the sperm). He affirms that the virgin birth is a matter of faith, and a commitment to the miraculous, and is thus beyond the usual bounds of historicity and experience.

By direct contrast, John Dominic Crossan argues that we must consider 'the virginal conception of Jesus to be a confessional statement about Jesus' status not a biological statement about Mary's body'.[8] At best the story of Mary and Gabriel and Joseph's dream is later retrojection and at worst deliberate deception. Crossan is committed to allowing cross-cultural anthropology and historical critical study to inform his reading of the New Testament.[9] That means using insights gained from scholars of the ancient near eastern traditions and the first-century Mediterranean culture to explain what may be going on within the exciting narratives around Jesus' birth. He proceeds from the assumption that women do not become pregnant without male sperm, and that the virgin birth is, therefore, outside the realms of normal human experience. Crossan believes that appeal to the miraculous should only be made when there's not another plausible explanation available. He is troubled by the likelihood or probability of Jesus being so unique within a first-century near-eastern context and yet the story of his birth being so absent from the oral tradition that preceded the written scriptures. Surely the shepherds would have talked about it? And the Magi? And Mary's family and close friends? Surely St Paul would have thought it important? Crossan's point is that if these extraordinary claims can be explained another way – such as later interjection by writers who wanted to remove doubt about Jesus' status in God's salvation plan – then that is most likely to have happened.

Crossan's alternative hermeneutic, he argues, makes sense if Jesus' ministry is construed as that of a prophetic preacher, heralding a political revolution. According to the argument, this understanding best reflects the context in which Jesus lived and the nature of his death. Jesus' political role is significant in Scripture; he was opposed by those in power – both the Jewish authorities and the Roman overlords – and stood up for those who were oppressed. Could it be, then, that Jesus was part of a resistance movement; a political radical wanting to see the end of the Roman occupation, the overthrow of the Jewish authorities who appeased them at the expense of the poorest Jews, and the establishment of the Kingdom of God?[10] Crossan contends that the earliest Christian communities were responsible for transforming Jesus from this revolutionary figure into a religious figure; an object of devotion instead of cultural deviant. They were 'the cultured few … the elites' who could write gospels, epistles and hymns that shaped the community's thinking.[11] In such a view, the 'original' Jesus did not require a virginal birth and so it must be a later interpolation. On this basis, Crossan critiques every tradition in which Jesus is described as anything other than a peasant-class, illiterate, skilled worker with a radical political vision – including the Nicene and Chalcedonian theologies which have become standards of Christian orthodoxy. Thus, all records of Jesus' miracles, healings and amazing teaching were added later to help re-paint a picture of Jesus Christ that suited the community. Crossan is blunt about this:

> Scenes, in other words, such as Luke 2.41–52 where Jesus' youthful wisdom astonishes the learned teachers in the Temple at Jerusalem, or Luke 4.1–30, where his adult skill in finding and interpreting a certain Isaiah passage astonishes his fellow villagers in the synagogue at Nazareth, must be seen clearly for what they are: Lukan propaganda …[12]

But something more significant than propaganda is going on here, in Crossan's analysis. The incarnation and virgin birth are not only fake news, they undermine the humanity and earthiness of the real historical Jesus in favour of some theological idol created for an over-pious community. The propaganda is relevant, properly speaking, because it tells us about the earliest Christian communities and the means by which they constructed their identity. In Crossan's view, the virgin birth stories tell us nothing about Jesus' true humanity.

Somewhere between these two positions, Andrew Lincoln offers us a middle ground that keeps confessional orthodoxy while taking historical criticism seriously. Like Crossan, he engages with the virgin birth tradition as it might be historically situated, but he does not share the goal of charging the earliest Christians with disingenuousness. Instead he explores what the mythic stories of Christ's birth were intended to communicate, and what may have been the overarching *purpose* of the community's creative interpolations. Lincoln is concerned with the *meaning* of the credal claim rather than its biological factuality. Unlike Crossan, Lincoln affirms the doctrine of the incarnation and thus thinks that the infancy narratives are an effort to make sense of that claim. They discuss ontological rather than biological themes, helping the gospel audiences make sense of who Jesus is as saviour:

> These birth narratives are composed in a way that not only expresses later Christological belief, but also anticipates what will happen to Jesus himself and to the message about him. There will be rejection and persecution by Jewish leaders, adumbrated by Herod's attempt to destroy this child (Matt. 2.1–18) and by Simeon's prophecy to Mary that her child will be 'a sign that will be opposed' (Luke 2.34–35). At the same time there will be acceptance of the message on the part of Gentiles and so Matthew has the magi come to pay homage to the child (Matt. 2.1–12), while Luke has Simeon say of this child that he has seen God's salvation 'which you have prepared in the presence of all peoples, a light for revelation to the Gentiles (Luke 2.30–32).[13]

For Lincoln, the gospels are craftwork, carefully structured to reflect back into Christ's past something about his identity that was only known after the resurrection: he is God (cf. Rom. 1.4).[14] And historical and literary criticism help us to see that the nativity story betrays its historic-construction, reflecting the first-century belief that the 'corporeal substance' of human existence came from women.[15] Thus, Mary supplied the humanity and the Holy Spirit supplied the divinity in the traditional story. While what Matthew and Luke are trying to convey about Christ is true, as far as Lincoln is concerned, the manner in which they do so may not be: 'trusting them as divine revelation entails trusting their witness to the significance of Jesus and does necessarily mean taking them literally as straightforward, historically accurate accounts'.[16] Lincoln is committed to the notion that Christ is God, but argues that this is revealed primarily at the resurrection, and the birth narratives are there to encourage us to believe it rather than to explain how it is possible. In other words, the nativity story makes ontological rather than biological claims about *Jesus Christ* not Mary. They are aiming to tell the truth about him, and use creative methods to do so. This truth is to be believed, but the means of its communication need not be.

These three approaches make quite divergent claims when it comes to the virginity of Mary, but all three agree that the real focus of the tradition is not Mary but Jesus: it is about establishing his credentials as saviour. While Crossan challenges the received tradition when it comes to Jesus Christ, Crisp and Lincoln affirm the credal claim about Christ's divinity and the incarnation. For all three it really matters that Jesus is human. Though his views sit largely outside the orthodox teachings of the Church, for Crossan the humanity matters because it is the most real and honest part of the New Testament story, earthing the gospel of love and inclusion in real achievable terms and fending off the problematic tendency to make Christ super-human or distant from real humans because of his divinity. For Crisp and Lincoln, who affirm the credal claims about Christ's divine-human identity, the humanity matters because it is central to the incarnation which is the means of salvation. Only God can save, so it matters that Jesus is divine, but this God must take onto himself the humanity that he seeks to redeem, and so he must also be human. If not, then nothing and no-one may be saved. Emphasis on the humanity of Jesus in the context of the virgin birth is a helpful step into considering the ethical implications of this article of the Creed.

## The Importance of a Really Human Jesus

Why does the humanity of Jesus matter? According to the writer to the Hebrews it was Christ's being human that made salvation a real possibility. Jesus is not only Son of God, but also the 'Great High Priest' who is able to sympathize with human weakness because he 'in every respect has been tested as we are, yet without sin' (Heb. 4.15). The writer goes on to compare Christ to the priests of the Old Testament, offering gifts and sacrifices for sin, and dealing gently with sinners because of their own frailty (Heb. 5.1–2). There's no hint here that the writer thinks Jesus is sinful like other priests – he does not need to make a sacrifice for himself as well as the people – rather Jesus' uniqueness is his radical empathy (rather than sympathy) as a fellow human creature who had the same weaknesses and temptations and frailties and yet did not sin. It was his sinlessness that indicated his status as God's Son (Heb. 5.5b). The writer to the Hebrews thus presents us with a tentative notion of divine-human agency in Christ, a scriptural prefigurement of the hypostatic union: the human High Priest sympathizing with those on whose behalf he stands before God, and the divine Son coming from God to draw near to the world to save it. Both natures are integral to the salvation of the world.

The mystery of Christ's full humanity and full divinity was the subject of much debate in the earliest centuries of the Church. It was not until the Council of Chalcedon agreed a common *definition* of Christ's identity in the fifth century that some sense of common orthodoxy was achieved. The definition was published with supporting theological documents such as a letter from Leo I, Bishop of Rome, to Flavian, Bishop of Constantinople, in about the year 449, sometimes called 'The Tome of Leo'.[17] The epistle is a theological excursus clarifying and expounding Leo's understanding of the scriptural witness to Christ's person and work. It was sent to Flavian to maintain friendly relations between the two bishops after a Constantinopolitan presbyter called Eutyches fled to Rome for refuge. Eutyches had been a celebrated interlocutor at the Council of Ephesus in 431, where he challenged his then Bishop, Nestorius, for overemphasizing the distinctiveness of the natures in Christ to such as extent that he could attribute certain activities to the humanity and others to the divinity. The argument was centred on the title 'Mother of God' and whether it could be appropriately applied to Mary. Eutyches, agreeing with the Bishop of Alexandria, Cyril, insisted it could. He argued that Jesus Christ was a singular identity with two natures, and thus that it was appropriate to call Mary the Mother of God because what she birthed was a fully divine human person. Twenty years later, however, Eutyches was accused of heresy by Bishop Flavian for suggesting that the divine nature somehow overwhelmed the human nature, or at least was the more significant of the two in terms of Jesus' will. Pope Leo wrote in order to maintain good relations with Flavian, to explain their points of convergence around the Nicene Creed, and to distance himself from Eutyches' teaching. Like the writer to the Hebrews, Leo argued that the principal purpose of the incarnation or in-humanization of the Son was for 'the restoration of humanity which had been led astray' and furthermore that this salvific work was necessary because 'we would not be able to overcome the author of sin and of death unless he whom sin could not stain nor death hold took on our nature and made it his own'.[18] The humanity of Christ was the means of salvation, and therefore only a fully human saviour could save human beings in their entirety. Leo certainly understood this in light of virginal conception and birth, stating that the 'virginal conception is something that God effects' to ensure the full humanity *and* divinity, 'the Holy Spirit made the virgin fertile, but the substantive body derived from her body'.[19] In doing so, Leo was keen to say, the divine Son was not diminished, but the humanity that he adopted in the incarnation was enhanced (cf. Phil 2.6–11). And this humanity that Christ exalts is common to all human beings, despite its miraculous conception. Leo was careful to avoid any sense that the virgin birth could impair the possibility of salvation, after all, all humanity originates in God's creative work. Thus there is no form of humanity that is beyond divine reach. Indeed, the miraculous conception was necessary to ensure that what was saved was genuinely human – passing through ordinary human gestation, growth and development, and birth. This ordinary humanness of Jesus Christ is emphasized further by Leo when summing up, 'let him [Eutyches] acknowledge the flesh of the one whose death he affirms ... let him not deny the one whom he knows to have been capable of suffering was human being with our sort of body ...' It's easy to pass by this statement, but it is worth noting that Leo, and subsequently the Council of Chalcedon that promulgated his letter, thought Christ's humanity was not distinct from ours in his ability to suffer and feel pain. This is Leo's proof that the humanity is genuine, and that it effects real salvation for those who will believe.

*****

If we assume with Crossan, Crisp and Lincoln that the meaning of the virgin birth tradition relates primarily to the identity of Christ, and in particular the full humanity that was his because of it, then we might ask what is implied by this commitment for an integrated ethics of discipleship. One way to locate the discussion is to consider Jesus' humanity in relation to another current ethical debate about disability and humanity. It is an important discussion not simply because of its relevance to our twenty-first-century culture, but because it forces us to reckon with the kind of humanity that we associate with Jesus. Many presentations of Christ are stereotyped by the stained-glass window I used to see on a regular basis when I was a vicar: Christ is perfectly shaped, with sallow complexion and serene expression. He is usually muscular, well built, and strong but his body has been rendered weak and incapable by nails and wood and thorns. Depending on the age of the glass, his expression might show the pain of the situation, or it might be borne by those gathered at the foot of the cross.

When we hold such images of death alongside the virgin birth narrative, it is possible to discern a common effort within Christian history to distance Christ from any personal sin or stain and the subsequent accompanying brokenness. He did not inherit sin from his virginal mother, and when he did encounter other peoples' sinfulness its effects on him were deadly. Read the wrong way, such artwork and story-telling suggests a connection between physical weakness and sinfulness. The perfect Christ is strong and fully human until he is broken by sin on the cross (2 Cor. 5.21) at which point his body is incapacitated and wrought with suffering and pain. The telling of the story juxtaposes them: on the one hand sinlessness, bodily perfection, and fulness of life; on the other hand, sin, brokenness, and physical disability. And, of course, in some parts of the Church people believe that wholeness and healing come as a sign of the gospel, and therefore disability indicates a problem of faith or the presence of unconfessed sin. It's how the disciples reacted to disability in John 9. Jesus came across a man born blind, and the disciples ask him 'Rabbi, who sinned, this man or his parents, that he was born blind?' (John 9.2). It's an offensive question to our ears, as if disability is either blameworthy or a divine punishment. But to Jesus' disciples it was part of a wider religious understanding of the fabric of things, and thus part of their explanation of imperfection and suffering. Jesus' response could be equally offensive, however: 'Neither this man or his parents sinned; he was born blind so that God's works might be revealed in him.' It is reassuring that Jesus does not buy into the standard pattern of relating disability to sinfulness, but in challenging that he suggests the utilization of the man's obvious suffering for the greater glory of God. To many it sounds cruel. But there is also affirmation in this moment: Jesus does not deny the man his time or effort, and indeed he heals him. (I will come back to the topic of suffering and Jesus in the next chapter.) The healing is not absolute: we assume that the man did eventually die, but for that moment in time Jesus rehabilitated the man.

Of course, juxtaposing Christ's perfect humanity and thus

perfect physical and mental capacity with the brokenness and sinfulness of the world and thus with disability and suffering is not the only way to structure this discourse. More recently serious theological attention has been paid to the question of disability and how it should be understood in the light of the gospel.

## An Alternative Approach to Disability

In his revolutionary approach to disability, Hans Reinders proposes a different Christian response to the issue with significantly different attitudes to Christ's humanity. He locates Christian understanding of disability within the idea that humanity and personhood are realized when they are enacted relationally. The theological basis for this is the doctrine of the Trinity[20] and his basic point is that the relational God created people for relationships too. Relationality is not based on preference but on presence: those fellow human-creatures we encounter are alongside us for relationship. In this simple readjustment of thought, Reinders challenges any notion (latent or otherwise) that what makes a human life worthy of another's time, effort or attention is the extent to which the person contributes to society. It challenges the idea that her value is constructed or located in something the person does rather than who they are as God's creature. Reinders opposes any assumption that lives only have meaning and worth within particular cultural parameters, making participation in those cultural norms necessary, since for those whose ability to participate is hindered or impaired by disability, it is difficult to ascribe meaning and purpose in such circumstances. If society values lives based upon work, status, paying taxes, autonomy, independence, etc., and such things are impossible for people with profound disabilities, then it raises significant questions about the value of their existence.

In a particularly powerful discussion of Stanley Hauerwas'

work on cognitive disability, Reinders asks whether it is necessary to assume that there is a 'categorical difference' between disabled people and everyone else[21] and agrees with Hauerwas that such is only the case if our common humanity is forgotten or misinterpreted. To argue *for* the categorical difference is to argue that disabled people are not as human as other people. Such arguments *have* been made, but not usually by Christians. The Australian philosopher and ethicist, Peter Singer, has (in) famously argued that 'the fact a being is a human being, in the sense of being a member of the species Homo sapiens, is not relevant to the wrongness of killing it; it is, rather, characteristics like rationality, autonomy and self-consciousness that make the difference'.[22] The definite implication, which Singer develops in the book, is that people with disabilities that do not fulfil his definition of 'normal' human being may be deemed killable by society. This is because they are dependent upon others, initially their parents and then the state, and dependence is a hindrance to mature human adulthood. In particularly severe cases, Singer argues that the sentience of infants should be disregarded as a reason for preserving their lives if they will bring unhappiness to the parents or excessive dependency on the state. Underlying all of this is the extrinsic value attributed to profoundly disabled people, i.e. that their value depends on the context, culture and disposition of the society in which they exist.

In contradistinction, because of the incarnation Reinders thinks that the essence of human being is intrinsic and universal, and is valuable in itself. Though it is not necessarily obvious to us, there is such a thing as common humanity, in which all disabled and non-disabled people share, because of the creative and redemptive work of God. Reinders points to the 'relationship that the triune God maintains with humanity through the economy of salvation'[23] to demonstrate his point. In Jesus Christ, God the Son took on humanity, and that must also include disabled humanity or else it would suggest that disabled people are not human or not the object of Christ's redeeming work. But this seems patently obviously wrong, given Jesus' ministry among the sick, the disabled, the outcast and the stigmatized.

Reinders extends the insight arguing that if human being is God's idea, and its fulfilment is God's idea and commitment, then what a full or normal human being looks like is also God's idea. He summarizes, 'theologically speaking we are truly human because we are drawn into communion with God the Father, the Son and the Holy Spirit'.[24] Human beings are not worthy because of their ability, but because of God's grace. This metaphysical context matters; it helps Reinders establish the reference points for human value and worth. Relationship with God is the *telos* for which human beings were made; it is the meaning and purpose of all existence. This raises a question: does profound disability hinder the possibility of such a relationship? While we might think it difficult from our human perspective to be friends with someone who has a profound disability, Reinders flips the question to consider whether God would make such an offer to be friends with someone who is profoundly dependent and in need, and who has little to offer in return. If 'friendship' were purely about self-satisfaction then we might think it difficult; but the kind of friendship God offers is not because God is lacking something that human creatures might provide. On the contrary, God's friendship is grace and thus freely given. That means it is offered regardless of our willingness to be friends in return (Col. 2.13, Eph. 2.5), and it alone is the basis of the Christian life:

> The moral life from a Christian perspective is a response to the continuing offer of God's friendship that always precedes human action. This means, among other things, that our ways of dealing with other people are always a response to God's ways of dealing with us. Christian morality displays a three-way logic, not a two-way logic: it does not prescribe how to treat the other person, but rather how to treat the other person as a way to respond to how one is treated by God.[25]

Reinders' point is that in relation to God humans are utterly dependent and in need. Their friendship is not equal and opposite to God's. Nonetheless humans are valued, not because of what they give but because of who they are intrinsically as creatures, and who they are becoming in Christ. This value is expressed in the mission of God in Christ. Therefore, the same gospel regulates human interaction: we are in no position to decide and judge one another's value, nor to belittle one another for varying degrees of contingency and dependence. Before God, humanity stands in solidarity. But more than that, Reinders argues that this is not a place of impotence or absolute weakness. To depend is part of the created order; it is the essence of relationship. Christians believe all of life is contingent: God is the originator and the perfector of creaturely existence. Human beings have been created for mutuality and relationship, and the proof of this is the human participation in God's triune, eternal relationship.

## So What?

What does this imply for an integrated ethics of discipleship? One obvious point is that if those people who are regarded as disabled are nonetheless friends and givers and receivers of love as any other human being, then they should be accorded the same dignity and respect as all human beings. John Swinton argues that one way to do this is to capture the African sense of *ubuntu* theology, or community theology.[26] The idea here is to flip the usual western pattern of conceiving of self as individual-in-relationship on its head, and preferring instead to understand human beings 'to be constituted as individuals through relationships and affiliations to other individuals, communities and ultimately to God. Within this worldview, personhood is not an individual possession. It is a gift bestowed on others within community'.[27] Communities of this sort cannot afford to be exclusive or limited in scope, or let barriers and blockages to full community exist without challenge. To do so would be to undermine the *gift* that each person is to the other within God's economy, and to warp the relationality that is integral to creation. Commenting on Genesis 1–2, Swinton argues, 'from the beginning, interpersonal relationships were vital for identity and humanness. Human beings were created for relationships … and ultimately it is God's relationship with human beings that is definitive and sustaining of human personhood'.[28] The sense of self that is often sought by western individualism is not really possible; we know ourselves only in community and in relationship.

Thus, we can infer, Christian ethics must put itself to work to ensure the full inclusion of those with disabilities and additional needs. This means the prospect of interruption, challenge and redirection. It also means opportunity to encounter God afresh. Underlying the requirement is a theology of friendship, in which members of the Christian community commit to one another under God, to seek one another's wellbeing, and to pursue one another's good. This is precisely what was entailed, for our good, in the incarnation. Such a friendship is not about only caring for those who are like us, share our interests, or offer us something in return; such an account of friendship is informed by the movement towards the radically different 'other'.

At a basic level this movement means enabling one another's participation in common human life, so that we can be with each other in the same physical spaces.[29] There's little point worshipping in church buildings that prohibit the inclusion of those with wheelchairs, or who are hard of hearing, or where the ground isn't level, or seating is inappropriate. These are basic requirements – what the Word Heath Organization Report on Disability calls 'enabling environments' – and many of them are enshrined in law to preserve the rights and dignities of disabled people, to enable them to participate in democratic systems, and to contribute to their sense of wellbeing.[30] One helpful resource for thinking about this in relation to the Church is a disability resource book produced by *Inclusive Church*.[31] The book includes both theological reflection on the place and roles of disabled people within the life of a congregation and community, but also signposts additional resources for equipping churches to be inclusive. There is a suggested checklist of key points to note in the process of becoming inclusive of disabled people, and a list of links to useful organizations as well as further reading. This is all practically useful; but a theological account of inclusion and participation must involve more than that. If others are gifts to be received within God's economy, and I too ought to be thought of as a gift to others, then there is a challenge to be open to the impact that Christians of different backgrounds, experiences, ethnicities and abilities will have on one another. Openness means genuine vulnerability and challenge. It may also means change and transformation.

Swinton's point about community is again helpful. The Church is a community that is externally generated; it is a work of the Holy Spirit who gathers people around Christ. Christians do not choose who the Spirit gathers, and therefore do not choose who is part of Church. Though in practice people are often excluded because what is done in the community is inaccessible or culturally distant. That means that in some cases those with disabilities who might be part of the Church – and thus would be those whose wellbeing we would pursue if we knew them – are not yet able to share in the common life of the people of God. Making participation possible and real for disabled people begins by seeing common humanity in Christ, and thus the radical power of recognition.[32] Jesus' humanity is the humanity of all people: his suffering and pain and limitation was not a negation of being human, but his radical participation in our human existence. Even the post-resurrection Christ still bore the wounds of crucifixion.

In the episode of the healing of the man born blind, Jesus first saw the man and then healed him (John 9.1). It was a pattern oft repeated in his ministry: seeing people who might otherwise be overlooked, excluded and marginalized as human beings worthy of his time and attention. The early Church was made up of people such as that, and its expansive reach was multi-

ethnic, multi-lingual and multi-cultural.[33] The humanity that
Christ assumed at the incarnation was not so particular as to
exclude or diminish some real human experiences. Indeed, he
is the everyman figure, in whom all that it is to be human and
all that human could be, come together. An integrated ethics of
discipleship will do the same; it will see people on the margins
as equally human and equally valued and loved by God, and
it will also make every effort to include rather than exclude.
That means breaking down practical barriers to participation,
but more radically it means being impacted and shaped by their
presence as gifts from God. It may even mean relocating to the
margins of our world as Christ did.

## Questions

What might it do to your worship to think carefully about
Jesus' humanity in relation to modern concerns about
diversity, including disability, ethnicity and sex?

How alert is your local church to the need to be accessible and
inclusive of people with a range of abilities? How might you
raise your church's theological awareness of its importance?

## Further reading

Herbert, Clare, John Hull and Wendy Bryant, *Disability:
The Inclusive Church Resource* (London: Darton, Longman and
Todd, 2014).
Reinders, Hans, *Receiving the Gift of Friendship: Profound
Disability, Theological Anthropology, and Ethics* (Grand Rapids:
Eerdmans, 2008).

### Notes

1 On the importance of Mary in recent systematic theology see, for
example, Thomas Weinandy, 'The Annunciation and Nativity: Undoing
the Sinful Act of Eve', *International Journal of Systematic Theology*, Vol. 14.2

(2012), 217–32.

2 For more on history in relation to Christology see Leander Keck, *Who is Jesus? History in Perfect Tense* (Edinburgh: T&T Clark, 2001).

3 Traditional defenders of the virgin birth also agree on this point. See, for example, C.E.B. Cranfield, 'Some Reflections on the Subject of the Virgin Birth', *Scottish Journal of Theology* Vol. 41.2 (1988), 177–90.

4 Andrew Lincoln, *Born of a Virgin? Reconceiving Jesus in the Bible, Tradition, and Theology* (Grand Rapids: Eerdmans, 2013), ch. 1.

5 Oliver Crisp, *God Incarnate: Explorations in Christology* (London: T&T Clark, 2009); Oliver Crisp, 'On the Fittingness of the Virgin Birth', *Heythrop Journal,* Vol. 99 (2008), 197–221.

6 Crisp, 'On the Fittingness', 197.

7 Crisp, 'On the Fittingness', 203.

8 John Dominic Crossan, *Jesus: A Revolutionary Biography* (New York: Harper Collins, 1994), 23.

9 Crossan's approach is not uncontroversial. Charles Cranfield has argued 'there is absolutely no possibility of anyone's being able to prove the historicity of the virgin birth (if it is historical) by historical critical methods'. Cranfield, 'Some Reflections on the Subject of the Virgin Birth', *Scottish Journal of Theology* Vol. 41.3 (1988), 177.

10 Crossan, *Jesus*, ch. 2.

11 Crossan, *Jesus*, 193.

12 Crossan, *Jesus*, 26.

13 Lincoln, *Born of a Virgin?*, 42.

14 Lincoln refers to the 'epistemological priority of the resurrection, which is the presupposition on which the birth announcements about Jesus' identity depend'. Lincoln, *Born of a Virgin?*, 269.

15 Lincoln, *Born of a Virgin?*, 196.

16 Lincoln, *Born of a Virgin?*, 244.

17 See Richard Norris, *The Christological Controversy* (Philadelphia: Fortress Press, 1980), 145–55.

18 Norris, *The Christological Controversy*, 146; 152; cf. 2 Corinthians 5.21.

19 Norris, *The Christological Controversy,* 148.

20 Hans Reinders, *Receiving the Gift of Friendship: Profound Disability, Theological Anthropology, and Ethics* (Grand Rapids: Eerdmans, 2008).

21 Reinders, *Receiving the Gift of Friendship*, 203.

22 Peter Singer, *Practical Ethics* (Cambridge: Cambridge University Press, 1998), 182.

23 Reinders, *Receiving the Gift of Friendship*, 273.

24 Reinders, *Receiving the Gift of Friendship*, 274.

25 Reinders, *Receiving the Gift of Friendship*, 316–17.

26 Swinton, *Raging with Compassion*, 201–5.

27 Swinton, *Raging with Compassion*, 202.

28 Swinton, *Raging with Compassion*, 204.

29 Attending to this concern has been the great gift of the L'Arche Community and the work of Jean Vanier. See his *Community and Growth*

(New York: Paulist Press, 1990) and also *Our Journey Home: Rediscovering a Common Humanity Beyond our Differences* (Maryknoll: Orbis Books, 1997).

30 World Health Organization, 'Enabling Environments' in its *Report on Disability* (Geneva: WHO, 2011), 168–201.

31 Clare Herbert, John Hull, and Wendy Bryant, *Disability: The Inclusive Church Resource* (London: Darton, Longman and Todd, 2014). Swinton, *Raging with Compassion*, 217–21.

32 See David Gushee, *The Sacredness of Human Life: Why an Ancient Biblical Vision is Key to the World's Future* (Grand Rapids: Eerdmans, 2013), 110–15.

33 This is what John Kilner has called 'a better way forward' in his *Dignity and Destiny: Humanity in the Image of God* (Grand Rapids: Eerdmans, 2015), 327–30.

# 6

# 'Suffered Death and was Buried ...': Suffering

In recent years it has been on trend to criticize the Nicene Creed and its authors for an overemphasis on the arrest, trial and crucifixion of Jesus – what is called the *passion narrative* – over and against the significance of his life and ministry. The second article of the Creed moves from Jesus' having been supernaturally conceived and born of the Virgin to his condemnation under Pontius Pilate, his crucifixion, suffering, death and burial. For some Christians this has been problematic. Tom Wright has openly criticized what he regards as the glaring oversight of Christ's Kingdom ministry, suggesting that it is the reason why many contemporary Christians know little of the meaning of the gospels and regard them as less theologically significant than the epistles.[1] Whether this is a true caricature of modern Christianity may need evidencing further, but such arguments help to sharpen our focus on the Creeds' concern for Jesus' suffering and death. Of course, it is part of the historic location of the Creeds that they are less concerned with existing points of convergence and seek instead to establish orthodox teaching on divisive or theologically complex issues such as the doctrine of the Trinity and the two-natured personhood of Jesus Christ. Of particular importance is the way in which the credal jump from birth to death and resurrection mirrors the heavy emphasis in the New Testament epistles on Christ's passion with very little attention to or repetition of the life, ministry and teaching of Jesus beyond the gospels.

For precisely this reason, some have argued that the Jesus we encounter in the gospels is quite distinct from the Christ described in the epistles, such that St Paul and the other apostles might rightly be regarded as the founders of Christianity; a new religion built around Jesus, but not one to which Jesus himself would have subscribed or supported.[2] What troubles this kind of claim is the resurrection: the earliest Christians believed that they had encountered the resurrected Christ, and that the resurrection was a declarative statement about Christ and about God (cf. Rom. 1.4). As such, they did not think themselves to be doing something distinct from or inconsistent with the ministry of Jesus, but to be appreciating the full revelation of who Christ was and is, what that meant for their understanding of God, and thus for their understanding of themselves as God's people. And it is precisely from the vantage point of the resurrection that the suffering and death of Jesus took on greater significance such that it became the foundational story of the Church, sacramentally remembered in both baptism and Eucharist.[3]

## Christ's Suffering

The New Testament's presentation of the suffering of Jesus Christ has many layers. It is clear that there is a political element to the opposition he received from the religious leaders and existing authorities. Throughout the gospels the scribes and the Pharisees regularly appear like the pantomime bad guys to challenge, oppose, trap, intimidate and put down Jesus. Readers know that in every instance Jesus defeated them with a question, or by some miraculous demonstration, or by winning over the gathered crowd through astonishing teaching. As the gospel narratives progress there is growing agitation between Jesus and the religious leaders, and they eventually decide to kill him (and those who associated with him, cf. John 12.9–11). In John's description of the decision, it was the Jewish Council's fear of Roman persecution that led them to the decision; they were afraid that Jesus' message would start a revolution that could not be won (John 11.45–54). So, rather than work with Jesus they colluded with the Romans, and in so doing exposed their principal allegiance to maintaining their safe position within their corner of the Empire. They knew that those political overlords would oppose any uprising or rebellion, any talk of freedom or hope beyond the Empire. To that extent, Jesus suffered as a victim of political backroom dealings, a friend's betrayal (Matt. 26.14–16), and class snobbery as the bastard son of a jobbing carpenter who dared to challenge the educated elites of his day (cf. Mark 6.3; John 1.46).[4] In Matthew's account, their decision to kill him followed his miraculous healing of the man with a withered arm. Jesus had exposed the religious leaders' hypocrisy in serving God but not serving their co-believers: in failing to serve the latter, they were failing to truly serve the former. The religious leaders' fury in the narrative is palpable, and the scene ends with their plot 'to destroy him' (Matt. 12.14).

Jesus' itinerant ministry was also his means of survival: moving around from place to place, teaching and preaching, healing and serving, but also having no home of his own (Matt. 8.20; Luke 9.58). If the gospels were a Hollywood movie, then there'd be a tense soundtrack every time Jesus went near to Jerusalem, a place of pilgrimage and of spiritual significance but also a hotbed of politics and power in which he was most in danger and where he would eventually suffer and die. Jesus suffered as a religious and political radical, accused of blasphemy and considered a rebel, precisely because of the life he lived.[5] And this life was one of intentional identification with weakest and poorest; people who were normally societal outcasts found themselves welcome in his company: women, the sick, the disabled and sinners.

But the suffering of Jesus is not only political. John's gospel suggests at several key moments that Jesus knew about his forthcoming suffering, and that he did not try to prevent it. The theme of 'the hour of glory' guides John's readers to understand more and more of Jesus' identity and what his overarching mission might have been. It is associated with the unveiling of his purpose. Jesus first says it as a rebuttal to Mary during the wedding at Cana, 'Woman, what concern is it to you and me? My hour has not yet come' (John 2.4). At this point it is a strange claim that makes little sense, but as the gospel unfolds it is repeated always in relation to some wider purpose or larger understanding of his ministry: to his unbelieving family members who tried to cajole Jesus into a more public (and more dangerous) ministry, he rejected their challenge by saying 'my time has not yet come' (John 7.6), and then later on the cusp of arrest for blasphemy John tells us that the authorities were prevented from laying hands on him, 'because his hour had not yet come' (John 7.30). Only when Jesus arrived in Jerusalem again and briefed his disciples do we know and understand that the 'hour' for which Jesus came was his suffering and death:

> ... unless a grain of wheat falls into the earth and dies it remains just a single grain of wheat. But if it dies, it bears much fruit. Those who love their life will lose it, and those who hate their life in this world will keep it for eternal life ... Now my soul is troubled. And what should I say – 'Father, save me from this hour'? No, it is for this reason that I have come to this hour. (John 12.24–27)

> Now, before the festival of the Passover, Jesus knew that his hour had come to depart from this world and go to the Father ... (John 13.1)

> Father, the hour has come; glorify your Son so the Son may glorify you. (John 17.1)

Theologically speaking, Jesus' suffering and death is the goal and purpose of the incarnation. While political struggles were a feature of his ministry, as well as personal griefs and anxieties (caused by, for example, the effort of his family to undermine his ministry and the accusations of devilment by the scribes in Mark 3.20–30, the ignorance of his disciples in Mark 8.14–21, or his isolation in his time of need in Matthew 26.40), the overarching purpose was sacrificial and vicarious suffering. As Hans Urs von Balthasar has described it, the incarnation is 'ordered to the passion'.[6] In other words, Christ's mission was to suffer and die.

Of course, the gospels do not end with the death of Jesus. The resurrection is the fulfilment of his mission: the overcoming of sin and death and the inauguration of renewed creation (2 Cor. 5.17). But the startling reality of Christ's death is only made clear after the resurrection; i.e. after his true identity is known (Rom. 1.4). And what mattered to the apostles was what Fleming Rutledge calls its 'living significance', by which she means the ongoing meaning and impact of this particular episode of suffering.[7] They made sense of this in the light of the Old Testament law. Jesus was regarded as a sin-bearing sacrifice, suffering and dying in a world marked by suffering and death for that world's own good: 'God made him who knew no sin to become sin, that in him we might become the righteousness of God' (2 Cor. 5.21, cf. Isa. 53.6,10).[8] His suffering was a sign of his cursedness, not because he was politically disruptive, but because he was taking the place of a divine-law breaker, and thus experiencing the disorderedness of the sinful creation: 'Christ redeemed us from the curse of the law by becoming a curse for us, for it is written, "cursed is everyone who hangs on a tree"' (Gal. 3.13, cf. Deut. 23.21). In the manner of a priest, Jesus offered up a sacrifice to God for the sins of the people, and out of solidarity with the people he became their saviour by suffering alongside them (Heb. 2.10), and offered the perfect sacrifice of his own life: 'Although he was God's Son he learned obedience through his suffering, and became the source of eternal life for all who will believe' (Heb. 5.8–9, cf. Lev. 16). Christ was treated unjustly and suffered unfairly, and 'bore our sins upon the cross' in order to liberate those who would follow him (1 Pet. 2.18–25, cf. Isa. 53.9). Thus the suffering of Christ belongs within a bigger narrative of salvation; that Christ who came to save, but experience the word of the world's brokenness and sin in order to subsume and destroy it. Hence St Paul's gloating, 'Where, O Death, is your victory? Where, O Death, is your sting?' (1 Cor. 15.55)

## Christ Suffers with a Suffering World

According to the scriptural witness, Christ's suffering was total: physical, emotional and spiritual. He was rejected by family (Mark 3.21), abandoned by his friends (Mark 14.10), lied about in public (Mark 14.56–58), suffered false trial (Matt. 26.59), beaten (Mark 15.19), mocked and spat upon (Matt. 26.67), and unjustly executed (Luke 23.4). He experienced a distancing from God (Matt. 27.45–46), and died in the prime of life amidst criminals, under the governance of a brutal Empire. It reflects in its depth and breadth the suffering of all human beings, from all contexts and walks of life across the whole of history: the pain, isolation, injustice, surprise, anger and anxiety that accompanies suffering. Yet, the New Testament condemns the brutality of this suffering while attesting its necessity. The resurrection is a vindication of Christ's sacrifice and a rejection of the finality of suffering and death. Suffering and death do not have the final word. Jesus really suffered because he was fully human in a world marked by suffering, but it was not the end of his story: on the third day he rose again. Christ suffered in solidarity with suffering human beings, and made possible the vindication of those who suffer. While this did not and does not remove the suffering of others, according to the Christian tradition it has made it possible and indeed necessary for a Christian account of suffering to oppose any sense of suffering's victory.

\*\*\*\*\*

What can be inferred from a theology of the suffering and death of Christ for an integrated ethics of discipleship? It is a challenging question, not least because the effects of Christ's sacrificial suffering and death cannot be replicated by any other human being: his vicarious work is unique. But the fact of Christ's suffering in the world and for the world is not beyond replication in itself, since there is an appropriate place for a disciple's imitation of Jesus (1 Cor. 11.1). That's not to say it must be sought after, but it is to acknowledge that suffering is a real part of human (including Christian) existence and some theological account needs to be given for it. One implication, then, that seems reasonable to explore in the light of the suffering of Jesus is the necessity for disciples to suffer with others. While there are several imaginable contexts in which this might happen, including political and social justice issues, it has a particularly important concern in the debate around the difficult question of suffering and quality of life, especially in relation to assisted suicide. Since this is one of the places where suffering is given its most potent moral worth in contemporary public discourse, I shall focus on it.

## The Debate

Actually defining what we mean by the phrase 'quality of life' is complicated. Where once it was a term used only within the medical profession, since the financial crisis of 2008 it has been marshalled in political, economic and educational contexts to give language to the growing concern for individual wellbeing and happiness. But the meaning of words gets stretched thin by imprecise overuse, and more recently scholars in the field of psychology have argued that there is no clear, coherent, objective definition of 'quality of life' available: it is used to do different things in different kinds of debates.[9] The one consistent feature they have observed is the 'subjective dimension' which allows people to define the concept on their own terms, often to meet their own ends.[10] Thus the best way to make sense of the idea is to observe it in action, in this case in the debates around suffering and assisted dying.

In the UK the debate around assisted dying in the last two decades has been particularly fraught. The current legislation dates to the 1961 Suicide Act, which states clearly that assisting or encouraging a person to complete suicide is illegal, and anyone found guilty of the crime should expect to serve a custodial sentence (to a maximum of 14 years). Three recent public examples of challenge to this law help us to see clearly the interweaving of the problem of suffering and the issue of quality of life.

The first is from October 2008, when Debbie Purdy appeared before the Crown Court to ask for clarification on the Suicide Act (1961) in relation to her husband. Purdy, who suffered from Multiple Sclerosis, was concerned that he would be prosecuted if he helped her travel to the *Dignitas* Clinic in Zurich, Switzerland. Purdy's concern was not about *whether* but about *when* to go to *Dignitas*: if her husband was likely to be prosecuted, she would have flown sooner rather than later while she still had physical capacity and was less dependent upon him for help. If it was unlikely, then she would remain in the UK for as long as her quality of life was satisfactory. The Court's verdict was published in August 2009. It requested clarification from the Director of Public Prosecutions (DPP) at the Crown Prosecution Service which was subsequently published in February 2010 (updated in October 2014) as a Policy Document outlining two key questions: (1) Would the prosecution be in the public interest? (2) What were the motivations of the assistant?[11] The DPP was clear that the Policy Document did not change the 1961 Suicide Act, but it did and does clarify the situations in which a public prosecution would be sought. In the event, Debbie Purdy did not fly to Switzerland to die, but died in a hospice in Yorkshire on 23 December 2014.

The second example is that of Tony Nicklinson. He suffered with locked-in syndrome following a stroke in 2005, and could move only his head and his eyes. He appeared before the High Court to ask to be given the assistance of a doctor in order to die (known as Physician Assisted Suicide, or PAS). In

Nicklinson's case, it would have been impossible to administer drugs himself because of the level of his paralysis, and so he needed the Courts to rule in order for a doctor or family member to administer the fatal medication. During the course of his campaign, he gave several TV and newspaper interviews to explain the sense of despair and indignity he felt at being trapped inside a body that didn't work. He described it as 'dull, miserable, demeaning, undignified and intolerable ...'[12] One of the TV interviewers, Cathy Newman, afterwards described her time spent with the Nicklinsons as tinged with 'overwhelming despair and hopelessness' and the 'longest, saddest interview' she had ever conducted, such was the level of his physical and emotional suffering.[13] The High Court ruled against Nicklinson in 2012. He died six days later after a hunger strike. His wife and daughter continued to campaign after his death and, together with two other families, brought an appeal against the original ruling to the Supreme Court in June 2014. The Supreme Court offered a nuanced verdict: they upheld the original ruling by a vote of 7–2, but in their summations the Bench observed that the issues with which they were presented were moral not legal, and as such outside of the remit of a Court: they, therefore, encouraged Parliament to once again review the legislation.[14]

The final example is that of 81-year-old Professor Emerita of Medieval English, Avril Henry, who killed herself in April 2016 using a cocktail of barbiturates that she purchased on the internet as a 'euthanasia pack'. Henry had been a long-term assisted dying campaigner, and member of Exit International, a lobby group who argue that suicide is a rational and viable option for those who do not want to live any longer, for whatever reason.[15] Henry regularly cited her chronic tinnitus, swollen ankles, developing incontinence and other medical ailments as depreciating her quality of life. In her detailed and articulate suicide note, she admitted that she had told her GP, friends, family and comrades at the local leisure centre of her intentions to kill herself for over a year before. It was a rational decision, made in full view of all facts about her physical deterioration.

Rather than continuing to weaken with age, and becoming a burden to others, she ended her life at the point of her own choosing when she felt 'life was complete'.[16]

Neither Debbie Purdy nor Tony Nicklinson nor Alice Henry were classified as terminally ill or dying. But each of them was experiencing chronic suffering and significant loss of quality, and indeed happiness, in being alive. Where for Nicklinson this was a sudden event following the stroke, for Purdy and Henry the added psychological turmoil of slow physical and mental deterioration that would occur before death meant that the option to kill oneself felt like a necessary consideration. Examples such as these have added weight to recent attempts to change the law. In 2005 it was the so-called Joffe Bill, or the 'Assisted Dying for the Terminally Ill' Bill, which was introduced to the House of Lords for discussion by Lord Joffe and subsequently rejected at the end of that parliamentary session by 148 to 100 votes.[17] Ten years later Lord Falconer attempted a revival of the Bill, this time in the light of Debbie Purdy and Tony Nicklinson's stories, presenting his Assisted Dying Bill to the House of Lords in the 2014–15 session and as a private member's bill in the Commons, proposed by MP Rob Marris. The substance of Falconer's Bill was much more robust and careful than Joffe's had been: only in circumstances of extreme suffering, with less than six months left to live (as agreed by two medical professionals), could suicide be permitted and aided by a doctor. The Bill made it to the second stage of reading before being defeated.[18]

What's important here is that in each case, suffering was so extreme and overwhelming that death was the means of regaining control over life; of rejecting further deterioration; of rebelling against the hopelessness of the situation; and of escape. In what follows I turn to consider two different Christian approaches to suffering.

## Christian Approaches to Suffering

One Christian approach to the kinds of stories I've just rehearsed is to say that compassion demands that those whose suffering is unbearable must be given the chance to end it. The most common advocacy is for assisted suicide.[19] For some, such as Karen Lebacqz, the key ethical point of Christianity is 'caring, compassion and the prevention of suffering in the face of death'. It is entailed within the command to love our neighbours, and pursue the common good. She frames it like this:

> Is it ever permissible not to use active euthanasia for the one who suffers with no hope of recovery? We would not hesitate to put an animal out of its misery. Why then would we not extend the same compassion to a human being? No, make that: the same compassion to mother or father, brother, a child, or friend. Surely if we care about another ... we would want to prevent that other's suffering?[20]

Hans Kung makes a similar case when he considers whether the suffering of another is the death that God desires, or is it an aberration from the divine will?[21] He is responding to the traditional sanctity of life argument which tends to emphasize the gifted-ness of human life, thus arguing that it is sacred and only to be ended by God. Küng is not rejecting the sanctity argument entirely, but pushing it to its furthest reaches and questioning its veracity: does sanctity simply mean that life must be lived at all costs, including those instances where it must be endured with diminished quality? What then is implied about God and the kind of life God gives if we expect and force people to suffer and endure chronic pain? Küng sums up his point:

> simply because human beings are human beings and remain so to the end, even when they are terminally ill (expecting death within the foreseeable period) or dying (expecting death in a short time), they have the right not only to a dignified life but also to a dignified dying and farewell, a right which may possibly be refused them by endless dependence on apparatus or drugs.[22]

Turning the argument on its head, Küng argues that precisely *because* life is sacred, we should seek euthanasia and assisted dying for those whose experience of this sacred life is undermined and destroyed by suffering.

An alternative approach is provided by Neil Messer.[23] He raises the question whether or not the framework for compassion and autonomy proposed by scholars such as Lebacqz and Küng is consistent with other Christian accounts of the human good. Is the total annihilation of suffering really the goal of Christianity this side of the eschaton? Might there be ways in which suffering is also an opportunity for something, as well as a challenge? Viewing suffering this way is not some sadistic trend, but takes seriously the way the suffering of Christ models for us the necessary approach to a Christian understanding: sometimes suffering has the potential for a meaning and purpose that we cannot see or understand. In which case the idea of endurance might be more appropriate than annihilation.

Messer roots his observations in St Paul's account of his thorn in the flesh in 2 Corinthians 12, which the apostle described as 'a messenger of satan to torment me, to keep me from being happy. Three times I appealed to the Lord about it, that it would leave me, but he said: "My grace is sufficient for you ..."' (2 Cor. 12.7–9). Scholars are divided about the exact nature of the 'thorn' – ideas including physical illness, blindness and persecution – but there is agreement that the suffering inflicted was real. This is clearly suggested by his appeal to God to take it away. What is instructive for Messer and for this wider debate is that St Paul comforts himself in response to God's promise of grace, to be 'content with weakness, insults, hardships, persecutions and calamities for the sake of Christ; for when I am weak, then I am strong' (2 Cor. 12.10). He does not have these things taken away, but is somehow better prepared to deal with them by considering them from the perspective of God's love and the grace he has experienced in Jesus Christ. Messer explains:

his thorn in the flesh was both a real and a terrible evil *and* an occasion by which he has experienced God's love and empowerment more fully than before ... the vision of suffering, love, and the good implied by this text suggest that those seeking to argue in Christian terms are not entitled to conclude that the love of my suffering neighbour requires me to kill her if that is the only way her suffering can be stopped.[24]

In orientating the question this way, Messer invites Christians to think of human life as real life, even in the midst of suffering, not because of the quality of our happiness in the midst of pain but because of Christ's concern for those who suffer. This concern was manifested not in rejection or avoidance, but by Christ's own endurance of suffering – even to death on a cross (Phil. 2.5–11). Again, this is not to ignore the negative effects and impact of suffering, but to deduce a way through suffering by seeing the peculiarities of present suffering in the light of a bigger theological narrative of grace. In framing suffering in this way, Christians are helped to see beyond it, to locate it appropriately in the bigger Christian story, and to change our attitude towards its finality. The pain is real, and must be affirmed as such, but its power is limited.

## Suffering with Those who Suffer

The ethical dilemma here is not an easy one, and the prospect that heeding Messer's gentle warning not to rush into assisted suicide as a normative approach to suffering should not be taken as license to tell those who suffer to put up with it. Looking for the silver-lining is not my charism, and neither is it a theological virtue. But the challenge Messer highlights should be considered carefully: what might it mean for Christian communities to be 'the kind of communities that can give suffering human being the resources to endure pain and indignity'?[25] I take this to be the sort of question implied by the suffering of Christ. Jesus' passion and death does not bring an end to all human suffering; on the contrary his is real and genuine human suffering. But the wider biography of Christ includes his ministry and his resurrection. Telling the whole story relativizes suffering in relation to a host of other things that can and should be said about the substance, meaning and direction of a person's life such that it does not have the final word– no matter how tragic, painful or desperate the circumstances.

Introducing assisted dying in such circumstances removes from society the inconvenience of caring for those who suffer, of suffering with them, and of investing in social care that attends both to their medical needs *and* their emotional and spiritual needs.[26] It hides from the challenge to the Church to be the sorts of communities where people are cared for and supported no matter how costly that may be. Messer's invitation is to reimagine not only how we suffer, but how we walk alongside those who suffer in the light of the gospel.

## Questions

How do you think God wants us to relate to our own suffering as well as that of others? How do you know?

Do you think assisted killing is an option for Christians? Why?

What difference does the suffering of Jesus make to your thinking about human suffering?

## Further reading

Badham, Paul, *Is There a Christian Case for Assisted Suicide? Voluntary Euthanasia Revisited* (London: SPCK, 2009).

Messer, Neil, 'Beyond Autonomy and Compassion: Reframing the Assisted Dying Debate' in his *Respecting Life: Theology and Bioethics* (London: SCM, 2011), 212–27.

Rutledge, Fleming, *The Crucifixion: Understanding the Death of Jesus Christ* (Grand Rapids: Eerdmans, 2015).

## Notes

1 N.T. Wright, *How God Became King: Getting to the Heart of the Gospels* (London: SPCK, 2012). The US version of this book has the subtitle, *The Forgotten Story of the Gospels* which suggests more directly the problem with the creeds Wright addresses. It has received various responses, but of note is James K. A. Smith's critique, 'Kings, Creeds, and the Canon: Musing on N. T. Wright', *The Reformed Journal*, March 27 2012, https://blog.reformedjournal.com/2012/03/27/kings-creeds-and-the-canon-musing-on-n-t-wright/ (accessed November 2018).

2 On this see David Wenham, *Paul: Follower of Jesus or Founder of Christianity?* (Grand Rapids: Eerdmans, 1995).

3 On this point see, for example, Richard Bauckham's published Didsbury Lectures, *God Crucified: Monotheism and Christology in the New Testament* (Carlisle: Paternoster, 1998).

4 One of the great themes of John Dominic Crossan's work is the peasantry of Jesus and all that that implies for his social status and thus the impact of his ministry. See his *Jesus: a Revolutionary Biography*, ch. 5.

5 This point is made helpfully and consistently by Stephen Patterson, *Beyond the Passion: Rethinking the Death and Life of Jesus* (Minneapolis: Fortress Press, 2004).

6 Hans Urs von Balthasar, *Mysterium Paschale* (Edinburgh: T&T Clark, 1990).

7 Fleming Rutledge, *The Crucifixion: Understanding the Death of Jesus Christ* (Grand Rapids: Eerdmans, 2015), xvii.

8 See Murray Harris, *The Second Epistle to the Corinthians*, The New International Greek Testament Commentary (Grand Rapids: Eerdmans, 2005), 449–56.

9 See, for example, Barbara Barcaccia et al., 'Defining Quality of Life: A Wild Goose Chase?' in *European Journal of Psychology* Vol. 9.1 (2013), 185–203.

10 Barcaccia et al., 'Defining Quality of Life', 197.

11 Director of Public Prosecutions, 'Suicide: Policy for Prosecutors in Respect of Cases of Encouraging or Assisting Suicide' (2010/2014), www.cps.gov.uk/legal-guidance/suicide-policy-prosecutors-respect-cases-encouraging-or-assisting-suicide (accessed January 2019).

12 From §13 of the 'Approved Judgement between Tony Nicklinson and Ministry of Justice', www.judiciary.uk/wp-content/uploads/JCO/Documents/Judgments/nicklinson-judgment-16082012.pdf (accessed January 2019).

13 Cathy Newman, 'Locked-in Syndrome Man in Court Bid for Right to Die', 18 June 2012, www.channel4.com/news/locked-in-syndrome-man-in-

court-bid-for-right-to-die (accessed January 2019).

14 The Bench addressed this specifically, claiming that they could not 'usurp the function of parliament' by making moral judgements. See §151 of the 'Approved Judgement', www.judiciary.uk/wp-content/uploads/JCO/Documents/Judgments/nicklinson-judgment-16082012.pdf

15 See more at https://exitinternational.net.

16 This phrase has taken on greater significance in recent years, being the basis of a campaign by the 'My Death: My Decision' lobby group, who argue that choosing to die is a rational option which should be protected in law. See www.mydeath-mydecision.org.uk/about/ (accessed January 2019).

17 Lord Joffe, 'Assisted Dying for the Terminally Ill Bill' (2005), https://publications.parliament.uk/pa/ld200506/ldbills/036/06036.i.html (accessed January 2019).

18 Lord Falconer continues to agitate for change on this issue: Charles Falconer, 'The Law on Assisted Dying in Britain is Incoherent and Hypocritical', *The Economist*, 21 August 2018, www.economist.com/open-future/2018/08/21/the-law-on-assisted-dying-in-britain-is-incoherent-and-hypocritical (accessed September 2018).

19 See for example Paul Badham, *Is There a Christian Case for Assisted Suicide? Voluntary Euthanasia Revisited* (London: SPCK, 2009), and Karen Lebacqz, 'Reflection' in Therese Lysaught et al. (eds.), *On Moral Medicine* (Grand Rapids: Eerdmans, 2012), 1088–90. See also Harriet Sherwood, 'Desmund Tutu: I Want the Right to End My Life Through Assisted Dying', *The Guardian Online*, 7 October 2016, www.theguardian.com/society/2016/oct/07/desmond-tutu-assisted-dying-world-leaders-should-take-action (accessed August 2018).

20 Lebacqz, 'Reflection', 1089.

21 Hans Küng, 'A Dignified Dying', in Therese Lysaught et al. (eds.), *On Moral Medicine* (Grand Rapids: Eerdmans, 2012), 1090.

22 Küng, 'A Dignified Dying', 1091.

23 See his 'Beyond Autonomy and Compassion: Reframing the Assisted Dying Debate' in his *Respecting Life: Theology and Bioethics* (London: SCM, 2011), 212–27.

24 Messer, 'Beyond Autonomy and Compassion', 222–3.

25 Messer, 'Beyond Autonomy and Compassion', 223.

26 This is the sort of argument made by the *Care not Killing* alliance – an organization with 40 institutional members made up of disability groups, faith groups, healthcare professionals, media groups as well as members of the general public. See www.carenotkilling.org.uk.

# 7

# 'On the Third Day He Rose Again': Hope and Moral Vision

In this chapter and the one that follows, I turn from the concrete actions that may be inferred from or implied by the doctrinal commitments described in the Creed towards the dispositions that make Christian ethics Christian. I begin here with hopefulness, before turning to prayer and spirituality in Chapter 8. The aim of this chapter is to sketch the moral terrain and then in the subsequent chapter I'll consider how we might inhabit it.

When I was a curate, the vicar (my training incumbent) once asked me: 'What is the gospel?' We were sitting in the vicarage garden thinking through what would be my first ever solo funeral at the end of the week. It was not the question I was expecting: he was supposed to check that I knew which liturgy to use, or about the organist's propensity to arrive only ten minutes early (therefore, I shouldn't panic), or that I'd remembered to let the undertakers know I would be travelling in the hearse to the crematorium, or that I had a copy of the son's eulogy should I need to take over from him during the service if he's too overcome to finish. He asked me again. I was keen to please and not waste time, so I said the only thing that I was thinking: 'Jesus has been raised from the dead.' Fr Nicholas gave one of his usual wry smiles and completed the sentence that I had unwittingly left unfinished, '... and so there's hope. That's what you are to preach at the funeral. Resurrection hope. Don't be crass about it. But don't give the impression that we think death has the final word. It doesn't. Jesus is alive.' He poured the coffee and I thought about what he said. Fr Nicholas has taken probably thousands of funerals in his many years of priestly ministry. Our conversation was a gift. It has shaped everything I've ever done as a parish priest. I had already considered the sermon, but I was terrified: *How could I preach the gospel of repentance and forgiveness when people were grieving or when I was unclear about the destination of the deceased?* The conversation that followed in the vicarage garden focused on the difference between the gospel and the call to respond to it. The good news preached in the New Testament isn't 'repent and believe'. Rather, 'repent and believe' was the apostles' invitation to those who heard the good news, as a sign that they had received it, and continues to be the Church's invitation to those who would be followers of Christ. But it always *follows* the gospel as *response* to it. The gospel is something much more radical and much more scandalous: Jesus Christ has been raised from the dead. The last great enemy is defeated. And thus Christ has become the hope of all believers (1 Tim. 1.1) through the abiding presence of his Holy Spirit (Rom.15.13).

The resurrection is not the completion of the work of Christ. It is, of course, of enormous significance: there is no gospel without the resurrection of Christ from the dead. But it is not the last act of Christ's work. 'On the third day he rose again …' with yet more work to do. The biblical narrative describes Jesus' post-resurrection ministry and appearances, and the ascension to the right hand of the Father from where he intercedes for the world (Rom. 8.34). Indeed, the second article of the Creed reorientates worshippers from the past events of Calvary and the empty tomb, to the future events of the eschaton: 'he will come again in glory to judge the living and the dead'. In between these two moments of resurrection and second coming, Christ is ascended; a fully human creature seated at the right hand of the Father.[1] The ascension is an oft overlooked doctrine, perhaps because its liturgical season is so brief and occurs outside of the usual run of Sunday worship, and yet its claims are radical and potent. The resurrected human Christ is now at the right hand of God the Father.[2] That means there is a human being forever in the presence of God; a temporal creature within the courts of the timeless God. And this creature is God's Son.[3] Christians do not and never have believed that at the ascension Jesus Christ was redivided into some antecedent component parts of humanity and divinity, and that it was the divine Logos or Son that ascended into heaven leaving the body behind. Though it was common among some Gnostic thinkers at the time, it was roundly rejected by the early Church as heresy. To believe it is to deny the bodily resurrection. But more importantly to believe it is to upend the biblical witness to the hypostatic union. Rather, orthodoxy confesses that the same Jesus Christ who is fully God and fully human and was crucified as such, is now risen and ascended and thus carries redeemed humanity into the eternal fellowship of the triune God.[4]

To consider Christian hope is to think precisely within the in-between space, with Christ's resurrection behind us and Christ's return ahead of us. Christians must think both retrospectively to the resurrection of Christ and prospectively to the second coming of the ascended Lord in order to discover the meaning of hope in the present. Hope is 'rooted in faith's trust in a *future* perfection which *has been* promised and secured'.[5] The resurrection is, therefore, the inauguration of something, which the Church and world anticipates and awaits.[6]

## Resurrection Hope

Perhaps the most famous biblical instance of this interweaving of resurrection and hope is the crescendo of St Paul's first epistle to the Corinthians, in chapter 15. It is the most expansive apostolic teaching on the resurrection of Christ, and why it matters first for Christians and then the whole cosmos. The initial section of the discourse, vss. 1–11, consists of five different appeals that St Paul makes to the Corinthian Christians to believe the resurrection of Jesus and to reject those who would cause them to doubt it.[7] The first is an appeal to tradition, 'For I handed on to you as of first importance what I first received' (15.3), rooting St Paul's preaching on the topic in the earlier apostolic witnesses and thus giving proper weight and authority to his exhortation for the Corinthians to remain steadfast. The second is an appeal to Scripture, 'Christ died for our sins according to the scriptures, and that he was buried, and that he was raised on the third day according to the scriptures' (15.3–4), demonstrating that neither Jesus Christ nor those who bear witness to him speak contrary to the Old Testament – which is surely the scriptures that are in mind here (cf. 1 Tim. 3.16) – and thus establishing Christ's credentials as God's saviour. The third appeal is to eye-witness testimony, the earliest claim of this kind in Scripture, both to strengthen St Paul's claim but also to dispel any notion that the event in question was an esoteric occurrence for only an initiated few 'he appeared to Cephas, then to the twelve, then to more than five hundred brothers and sisters ...' (15.5–6). His fourth appeal is to his own testimony, with which the Corinthian Christians would be familiar, and which brought the idea of Christ's resurrection power much closer to home for them: 'Last of all ... he appeared to me ... unfit to be called an apostle, because I persecuted the Church of God' (15.9). And finally, St Paul appealed to the experience and testimony of the Corinthians, reminding them of how they had come to faith and perhaps wanting to elicit some spark within them, 'so we proclaim and *you have come to believe*' (15.11). The passage is eloquent and rhetorically interesting: St Paul moves from tradition, to scripture, to reason, to two kinds of experience (second-hand and first-hand), covering all the relevant bases to lay the foundations for the argument that follows. And what follows is explanation of Christian hope. Thus, for the earliest Christians, there was no hope if the resurrection of Jesus Christ from the dead was not true. It is only by establishing the necessity of belief in resurrection that St Paul could begin to speak about living hopefully.

Certainly, St Paul aims to provoke his readers at this point.

Having laid foundations, he attacks those who would continue to undermine the resurrection of Christ:

> if Christ has not been raised then our proclamation has been in vain and your faith has been in vain … If Christ has not been raised then your faith is futile and you are still in your sins … If for this life only we have hoped in Christ, we of all people are most to be pitied. (1 Cor. 15.3–4, 14, 17, 19)

Christianity is pointless without the resurrection; it is vain, futile and pitiful if the defining event is actually little more than a myth or, worse, a lie. St Paul believed that the resurrection has cosmic impact: it transforms the present and establishes a new future horizon. If the resurrection is not true, then there is no hope beyond our present circumstances, no possibility of overcoming trials and tribulations, and no remedy for the finality of death. 'But,' the apostle declares, 'in fact Christ has been raised from the dead' (15.20), and that changes everything.

> For since death came through a human being, the resurrection of the dead has also come through a human being; for as in Adam all die, so all will be made alive in Christ. But each in his own order: Christ the first fruits, then at his coming those who belong to Christ. Then comes the end, when he hands over the Kingdom to God the Father. (1 Cor. 15.21–24)

Already we are in the realm of eschatology with these verses. The resurrection of Christ anticipates the future resurrection of all people.[8] This is surely what is meant by the reference to 'first fruits', which is one of the many Old Testament cultic festivals. At the climax of the feast, the first fruits of the harvest would be presented to the priests as a sacrifice to God. During the festal procession, each worshipper would recite the story of inheriting the land as heirs to the covenant both to remind themselves of their identity as covenant people and to worship and glorify God who had redeemed them (Deut. 26.2–11). The first fruits were a portion of the whole harvest, an act of thanksgiving for God's faithfulness and of expectation that there would be more, suggesting that a much greater yield was to follow which was for the people to receive and enjoy. Here, St Paul suggests that the resurrection of Christ is to be understood in much the same way; it was the first portion of something much greater that is yet to come – the resurrection of all the dead. Christian hope is rooted in a past event but anticipates a future event that will be the fulfilment of God's promise. 'Then', the apostle tells us, 'comes the end, when Jesus hands over the kingdom to God the Father ...' (15.24). For now, Christians are caught in the in-between time.

## Eschatological Hope

The earliest preaching of the Church expected the imminent return of Jesus, what is often called the *parousia*, which would inaugurate the eschaton.[9] It is also the substance of the final clause of the second article of the Nicene Creed – 'he will come again in glory ...' Several times the New Testament writers reminded their readers that they were awaiting the saviour's return (Phil. 3.20), and his appearing in glory (Tit. 2.12–14), and there are suggestions that they wouldn't have long to wait (Ja. 5.7–8; 2 Pet. 3.12; 1 Tim. 6.14). Indeed, even the apocalyptic tradition believed that Jesus would 'come soon' (Rev. 22.20). And though, as I have suggested above, St Paul drew a clear line between the resurrection of Christ and the eschaton in 1 Corinthians 15, he gave much more detail in the earlier first epistle to the Thessalonians.[10] Indeed, it is such a theme in the epistle that scholars have claimed that 'eschatology is the best hermeneutical key for understanding first Thessalonians'.[11] Some of the eschatological material St Paul uses is reckoned to have significant antecedents and thus to reflect not only the apostle's ideas and teaching, but that of the earliest churches[12] who were still awaiting the coming of Christ nearly two decades after the ascension. St Paul would have been shaped by that expectation, and was clearly used to applying it. The particular pericope that sheds useful light on our discussion of eschatological hope runs from 4.13 to 5.11.[13]

The first section, 4.13–18, begins with a pastoral concern about death and mourning. St Paul appears to be responding to some worry about the fate of loved ones who had pre-deceased the second coming of the Lord. His response is to remind the Thessalonian believers of the gospel, 'since we believe that Jesus died and rose again, even so, through Jesus, God will bring with him those who have died' (4.14). The mode of argument here is both *analeptic* (looking backward) and *proleptic* (looking forward). St Paul begins with appeal to the now decades-old events of the death and resurrection of Jesus, and moves his argument forward from there. Precisely because Jesus died and was raised in the past, when this same Jesus comes again their loved ones will be raised with him. Because he *now* lives, they *will* live. Without the past event, the future would look different. Without the resurrection there would be no hope. The verses that follow are an expansion of that turn towards the future. The great expectation is for the day of Christ's coming, when 'the Lord himself, with a cry of command, with the archangel's call and with the sound of God's trumpet, will descend from heaven …' (4.16). It is known only because of 'the word of the Lord' (4.15), and thus it is a matter of revealed faith. That Jesus will 'descend' from heaven reverses his earlier ascent into heaven (Acts 1.6–11), and demonstrates the belief in the consistency of identity of the 'Lord' figure – the one who ascended is the one who was crucified and resurrected and who will descend. Furthermore, that 'we who are alive' (4.17) will see it and be caught up with those who are 'dead in Christ' (4.16b) suggests that the *parousia* was thought to be immanent. Significantly, at the heart of the picture painted by the apostle is relational intimacy: 'we will be with the Lord forever' (4.17b). The goal is not heaven or paradise or an abstract notion of peace or tranquillity. The goal is personal and corporate proximity to Jesus Christ. He is the focus of Christian hope, that 'we may live with him' (5.10).[14] Christ is, therefore, both the source of hope and the goal of hope.

The apostle is aware of the difficulty of having faith for the future in the present. Perhaps he is also plagued with the same questions about the time-delay to the *parouisa* that we might imagine others had after two decades of waiting. Certainly the second section of this discussion, 5.1–11, gives a steer on what to do between now and Christ's appearing. St Paul borrowed Old Testament prophetic imagery of the Day of the Lord (5.2; cf. Isa. 2.12, Joel 2.31, Amos 5.18–20) to describe the mystery surrounding Christ's arrival. Though in the Hebrew Bible it is a day of judgement or reckoning, even crisis,[15] for those who live in darkness (5.3), it is a day of peace and fulfilment for those who live in the light (5.4). For the Thessalonians it is a day to be celebrated rather than feared, in which the rule and reign of God will be established, and all shall be well (Dan. 12.12). With this in mind, the disciples at Thessalonica ought not be disappointed or downhearted but instead 'keep awake and be sober ... put on the breast plate of love, and for a helmet the hope of salvation, for God has destined us ... for salvation through our Lord Jesus Christ who died for us ...' (5.6–10). Hope is the direct result of God's salvific work, in particular Christ's death and resurrection; Christians, therefore, live in a present context that is conditioned by the future arrival of a previously crucified and resurrected Lord.

## Present Hope

Though the well-spring of hope is resurrection life, given and experienced through the abiding presence of the Holy Spirit, and its orientation is the *parousia* of Christ and his Kingdom, there is a present tense aspect to hope which is not idle anticipation. This is because hope is not an abstract theological idea. Christian hope is hope in the God of the gospel, and that God lives. It is thus hope in the God who is lively and at work in the present, and whose Spirit within us is the hope of glory (Rom. 5.5; Col.

1.27). This kind of hope, according to Jurgen Moltmann, takes on the form of *promise*: 'in it, the hidden future of God for the world is already present'.[16] The present-tense, promissory nature of hope only makes sense when we have mapped the metaphysical terrain retrospectively and prospectively, by looking backwards to the resurrection of Christ and forward to the *parousia*. What happens in between is condition by those two points: they are the whence and whither of the Christian existence. Present hope is thus a kind of *prolepsis* in which we decide and act in the present with a sense of direction, and thus meaning and purpose, as those who are promised to meet Jesus Christ.[17] But Christians view the present from an eschatological vantage point[18] because the Spirit of Jesus Christ – the one who is ahead of us – is sent into the lives of Christians now (Gal. 4.6; Rom. 8.9–12).[19] Thus a hopeful person is one whose approach to life is defined neither by self-assertion nor the self-promotion of the world around, but by the gospel's affirmation of human existence and the future good that awaits all of creation in the coming of Christ. This kind of hope is dynamic; it involves our movement towards that event both temporally and morally. It is this present activity of hopefulness that I shall explore as the principal posture of a Christian disciple.

*****

The implications of a disposition are of a different order from the other implications I have considered so far. Concrete decisions and actions such as commitment to conciliarity, the proper flourishing of non-human animals, political participation, openness and inclusivity, and fellow-suffering have been suggested as possible implications of the doctrines enshrined within the Creed, but something else is in mind when we think of hopefulness. Hope is a quality predicated upon some other action. A hopeful person is one who will, because Jesus Christ has been raised from the dead, dispose themselves in their decisions and actions to the eschatological vision of Christ's return. They will act presently in total commitment to that future, and what that future means for all creation. Hope of this kind is 'a significant spur ... to manifest God's Kingdom in daily life'.[20] It means 'action which seeks the fullest possible anticipation of our end'.[21] But, Christians who wish to be hopeful in this way are faced with a problem: it is not yet the *parousia* or the eschaton, and we do not know what the Kingdom will look like and feel like. Such things are known only to God, and may be discerned only in the power of the Holy Spirit. Christian disciples must be careful not to overreach and over-claim, to make the Kingdom fully present as if the Lord's Prayer were no longer to be prayed. I suggest, therefore, that the implications of hopefulness for an integrated ethics of discipleship take the form of three characteristics of ethical deliberation: imagination, self-criticism and mission.

Though it is possible to think of imagination and its cognates such as creativity as being at the opposite end of a spectrum from the concrete and systematized material of Christian doctrine, I don't think it is necessary to do so. Scholars have been divided about the place of imagination in theological reasoning – not least because it is putatively related to what is not, rather than what is. That is to say that imagination is often about introducing something new, conjuring-up or inventing, whereas traditionally theology has been understood as bearing witness to what already is true in Jesus Christ. Some have seen imagination as running contrary to the inherent *realism* of Christianity, seeing it as a kind of projection of the human psyche or desire.[22] Such rejection is built upon two mutual ideas: the first that imagination is not rational, and the second that our engagement with reality is primarily through sense-perceptions. The first objection matters because theology is inherently rational; it is about making sense of the biblical witness and giving coherence and shape to the Christian life lived in response to that witness. Any hint of irrationality undermines theology's work. The second objection matters because it relates to our common notion of reality and how we access it. If we introduce another means of engaging with reality beyond our common human experience it complicates things: it suggests some can make sense of what is real and some cannot. We end up with a problem of definition.

But more recent scholarship has begun to argue in favour of imagination. Several ecclesial theologians have taken the view that imagination is an activity of *redeemed* rationality put to the specific task of 'making or discovering connections' between the substance of our faith and the context in which it is to believed out.[23] To that extent its rationality is fideistic, but none the less logical. Imagination 'works' within boundaries set by Scripture and creed; it is not absolutely free. It thus cannot be the overreaching of human psyche or desire alone. Imagination is disciplined and shaped by the gospel. To imagine is to think inter-connectedly about identity, decision, and action with emphasis on the practical meaning of theological commitments. It is necessary in a context in which things change rapidly and require Christian thoughtfulness. Imagination is thus key to integrated ethics. Hopeful imagination means viewing the present and the future in an eschatological light, rooted in the death and resurrection of Jesus Christ. It means 'seeing everything that was, is, and is to come as related to what God the Father has done in his Son through the Spirit'.[24] Imagination names an all-encompassing way of viewing and making sense of the world. Imagination of this kind is closely related to vision: it involves 'seeing' and 'discovering' or making visible the coming Kingdom. It means *inhabiting* the in-between space appropriately.[25] Such an approach does not deny Christian realism, but on the contrary it is to say that what is most real is known only to God and must be revealed to creatures. Christians discern what is real and true, what is genuinely human action, in the light of Christ – who is both behind and ahead, as resurrected saviour and expected King. To be hopeful is, therefore, to imagine what to do and how to live as someone who anticipates meeting the resurrected and ascended Jesus face to face.

This leads to the second characteristic of hope: self-criticism. By this I certainly do not mean self-loathing or hatred. Self-criticism, I think, involves a healthy acceptance of one's limitations as a disciple. It is an extension or application of hopeful imagination, and means a willingness to be surprised, challenged and reorientated by the God of the gospel. Self-criticism refuses the tendency – present in the world since the garden of Eden – to presume access to knowledge and understanding which has been withheld from human beings. At its heart it is repentance, or a willingness to think again, to learn, to turn to Christ and to do so repeatedly. It means locating and making sense of one's own existence within the meta-narrative of expectation and longing for Christ's return; it means living in the light of that promissory hope. Truthful ethical discernment is impossible without self-criticism; unqualified self-affirmation is the root of idolatry. In this way, self-criticism is the personal application of hopeful imagination, asking of ourselves 'in what way do my decisions and actions reflect and inhabit the space between the resurrection and the *parousia*?' It is reflexive, but not self-interested. The concern of this kind of critical thinking is conformity to Christ.[26]

The third characteristic might be regarded as the outward version of the second. Where self-criticism is the reflective aspect of hopeful imagination, mission is its social aspect. It recognizes that Christian hope is for the world that God loves (John 3.16), rather than simply for the Church, and thus that hopeful imagination is for the transformation of society.[27] Commenting on the future-orientated calling of Christians described in Romans 12, Jürgen Moltmann explains, 'not to be confirmed to this world does not mean merely to be transformed in oneself, but to transform in opposition and creative expectation the face of the world in the midst of which one believes, hopes and loves.'[28] Hope thus requires the betterment of the world, and the Christian's pursuit of this in quiet rebellion against the *status quo*. Hopefulness is thus missional because it chooses the coming Kingdom now. In this paradigm, 'the call to discipleship of Christ … is the call to join in working for the Kingdom of God that is to come.'[29] This is the present-tense aspect of hope that I discussed earlier. Such promissory hope helps Christians to 'see the way the world currently runs as an insufferable, unacceptable affront' to God's intention.[30] Knowing this is essential is ethics is to make sense as a hopeful discipline. Kathryn Tanner explains,

> In this life, action that accords with the life-giving forces of God runs into the obstructions posed by our world as a realm of death – forces promoting impoverishment, suffering, exclusion, and injustice. One is called to counter such forces in the effort to bring in another kind of life.[31]

Both Moltmann and Tanner suggest in various ways that the coming of the Kingdom is something aided by Christian activity: the Church plays an active role in establishing the Kingdom's values in our contemporary world. I am not convinced that this is the case; the apostolic witness discussed earlier suggests that the *parousia* is something much more definite than potential, and not at all contingent upon human belief and practice. But it is also true that Christian hope is necessarily transformative. The Church's commitment to Christ's *parousia*, and thus its view that the future is realized only in Christ who is beyond us, radically implicates; believing it, trusting it and living for it will change us and, through us, the world in which we share.

## Summary

An integrated ethics of discipleship will be hopeful because Jesus Christ has been raised from the dead, has ascended to the right hand of the Father, and will come again in glory. Christians await and anticipate that return. A hopeful ethics will, therefore, be imaginative, making connections between our faith and the context in which we live it out, seeking to conform human existence both personally and corporately to the eschatological vision of humanity that Christ will realize at his coming. To live presently as those awaiting Christ's future is to be changed and transformed by the one for whom we wait. This is the work of the Holy Spirit, to which I turn in the following chapter.

## Questions

Do you ever think about the meaning and purpose of your life in relation to the bigger picture of God's plan and purpose for creation?

How does thinking in this way help you reframe your encounters with the world around?

What does it mean for you to be hopeful and how can that change the way you live?

## Further reading

Middleton, J. Richard, *A New Heaven and a New Earth: Reclaiming Biblical Eschatology* (Grand Rapids: Baker Academic, 2014).

### *Notes*

1 For more on this, see N.T. Wright, *Surprised by Hope: Rethinking Heaven, the Resurrection, and the Mission of the Church* (New York: Harper, 2008). And also, Matthew Levering, *Jesus and the Demise of Death: Resurrection, Afterlife, and the Fate of the Christian* (Waco, Tx.: Baylor University Press, 2012), ch. 3.

2 See Eph. 1:20; Col. 3:1; Heb. 1:3, 8:1, 10:12, 12:2; and 1 Pet. 3:22.

3 One of the first seriously theological questions my children, then eight and five years old, asked was in response to an ascension day service: 'who cooks his dinner when he's hungry in heaven?' asked my eight-year-old daughter. 'Never mind that,' worried my five-year-old son, 'is there a toilet up there?!' Problematic metaphysics and spacial metaphors aside, their appreciation for the bodily and therefore human resurrection of Jesus was significant.

4 Human participation in Christ's resurrection is a theme in Romans, where baptism is the enactment of that participation, cf. Rom. 6:6–11. See also Michael Thate, Kevin Vanhoozer, and Constantine Campbell (eds.), '*In Christ' in Paul: Explorations in Paul's Theology of Union and Participation* (Grand Rapids: Eerdmans, 2014).

5 John Webster, 'Hope' in his *Confessing God: Essays in Christian Dogmatics II* (London: T&T Clark, 2005), 197.

6 Christiaan Mostert explores the meaning of the resurrection as

inaugurated eschatology in 'The Kingdom Anticipated: The Church and Eschatology' *International Journal of Systematic Theology*, Vol. 13.1 (2011), 25–37.

7 For a more detailed examination see James Clark-Soles, *Death and the Afterlife in the New Testament* (London: T&T Clark, 2006), 70–72.

8 There has been significant scholarly argument about the meaning of the word 'all' in 1 Cor. 15:22. While commentators such as Gordon Fee have defended a limited notion, to be interpreted as something like 'all Christians' or 'all believers', others such as Charles Cosgrove note the imbalance that would be implied between 15:22a 'as in Adam all have sinned' and 15:22b 'so in Christ all shall be made alive' if the former interpretation were to be accepted. Though Cosgrove stops short of universalism (the idea that everybody will be saved in the end), the question cannot be ignored: if the first 'all' relates to the universal fall in Adam, the most natural and balanced reading of the second 'all' is universal salvation in Christ. See Gordon Fee, *The First Epistle to the Corinthians* (Grand Rapids: Eerdmans, 1987) and Charles Cosgrove, 'Hermeneutical Election' in his *Elusive Israel: The Puzzle of Election in Romans* (Louisville: Westminster John Knox, 1997), 26–45. Also of help on the issue of divine election is Stephen Williams, *The Election of Grace: A Riddle without a Resolution?* (Grand Rapids: Eerdmans, 2015).

9 For more detailed discussion see Paul O'Callaghan, *Christ Our Hope: An Introduction to Eschatology* (Washington: Catholic University of America Press, 2011), ch. 2.

10 General scholarly consensus is that Paul travelled through Thessalonica during his missionary journey, in the year c.48, and then composed the first letter around 50–51.

11 David Luckensmeyer, *The Eschatology of First Thessalonians* (Gottingen: Vandenhoeck & Ruprecht, 2009), 173.

12 See Alan Garrow, 'The Eschatological Tradition Behind 1 Thessalonians: Didache 16' in *Journal of New Testament Studies* Vol. 32.2 (2009), 191–215.

13 There is some scholarly debate surrounding this passage, and whether it should be regarded as a single unit or two distinct *topoi*. I am convinced by Luckensmeyer's conclusion that the thematic consistency of 4:13–5:11 compared to the surrounding text suggests it is one developing thought. See his thorough analysis of relevant literature in *The Eschatology of First Thessalonians*, 175–81.

14 John Webster argues that Christology is the substance of Christian hope, 'the Christian who hopes is one whose being is enclosed, determined and protected by Jesus Christ our hope', in his essay 'Hope' in *Confessing God*, 206.

15 See Luckensmeyer, *The Eschatology of First Thessalonians*, 276.

16 Jurgen Moltmann, *A Theology of Hope: On the Ground and Implications of a Christian Eschatology* (London: SCM Press, 1967), 326.

17 See Luckensmeyer, *The Eschatology of First Thessalonians*, 233.

18 See P.G. Villiers, 'The Eschatology of 1 Thessalonians in the Light of its Spirituality', *Acta Theological,* Vol. 28.1 (2008), 1–32.

19 See Gerald O'Collins, *Jesus Our Redeemer: A Christian Approach to Salvation* (Oxford: Oxford University Press, 2007), ch. 10.

20 J. Richard Middleton, *A New Heaven and a New Earth: Reclaiming Biblical Eschatology* (Grand Rapids: Baker Academic, 2014), 154.

21 Webster, 'Hope' in *Confessing God*, 213.

22 For a helpful summary of recent scholarly discussion see Kevin Vanhoozer, 'The Discarded Imagination: Metaphors by Which a Holy Nation Lives' in his *Pictures in a Theological Exhibition: Scenes of the Church's Worship, Witness and Wisdom* (London: Inter-Varsity Press, 2016), 17–48.

23 Vanhoozer, 'Discarded Imagination', 24.

24 Vanhoozer, 'Discarded Imagination', 27.

25 Vanhoozer, 'Discarded Imagination', 45–6.

26 For more on the rejection of idolatry see David Baker, *The Decalogue: Living as the People of God* (London: Apollos, 2017), ch. 2.

27 A really helpful overview of twentieth-century approaches to this theme is in Christofer Frey, 'Eschatology and Ethics: Their Relation in Recent Continental Protestantism' in Henning Graf Reventlow (ed.), *Eschatology in the Bible and in Jewish and Christian Tradition* JSOT Supplement 243 (Sheffield: Sheffield Academic Press, 1997), 62–74.

28 Jürgen Moltmann, *A Theology of Hope: On the Ground and Implications of Christian Eschatology* (London: SCM Press, 1988), 330.

29 Moltmann, *Theology of Hope*, 333.

30 Though Kathryn Tanner cuts across the historical/temporal aspects of eschatology to make the discourse primarily about the qualitative distinction between Kingdom and not-Kingdom, none the less her point about the ethical function of eschatology is helpful. See her *Jesus, Humanity, and the Trinity: A Brief Systematic Theology* (Minneapolis: Fortress Press, 2001), 119–124.

31 Tanner, *Jesus, Humanity, and the Trinity*, 122.

# 8

# 'The Lord and Giver of Life …': The Holy Spirit and the Christian Life

If hopefulness is the principal disposition of Christian ethics because the Christian life is lived between Christ's resurrection and *parousia and* these two points are guaranteed fixed poles within a Christian account of reality, then prayerfulness is what keeps us hopeful. Prayer is the mode of Christian navigation through this 'in-between' space and it is the Holy Spirit, 'the Lord and Giver of Life', who helps and enables Christians to do it.

The Christian life is pneumatic life. That's not some ethereal claim or pseudo-gnostic preference for the life of the spirit over the body. It summarizes and describes the theology of Christian existence: life lived in the power and under the influence of the third person of the Trinity. As the Pentecostal scholar Gordon Fee has summarized it, 'the whole of Christian life is a matter of Spirit'.[1] Noting this is important for two reasons. The first is that Christian *life* is real life as it is located concretely, with the daily interplay of identity, decision and action. That means that any thinking about it must reckon with the mechanisms for growing into and making sense of Christian identity, and the impact this will have on the shape of moral discernment and ethical practice. The second is that it is *Christian* life, and thus is it shaped and directed in relation to Jesus Christ. The adjective has theological and therefore ethical content. Those questions of identity, decision making and action are all conditioned in proximity to the Christ who is alive.[2] While at first glance this might seem to counter the claim just made that the Christian life is a spiritual life, it is important not to separate the persons of the Trinity and emphasize one at the expense of another. Doing so renders all our talk of God unfaithful. Theologically speaking, it is the Holy Spirit who enacts the proximity of Jesus Christ to his Church. This is because the Holy Spirit that Christians receive is the Spirit of the resurrected One (Rom. 8.9; 1 Pet. 1.11). The interplay between the Son and Spirit is a significant feature of trinitarian theology, and took the Church some time to express coherently.

The Nicene Creed of 325 limited the third article to 'And in the Holy Spirit' and it was only later that it expended to its present form at the ecumenical Council of Constantinople (381). The concern of those later bishops was that a full understanding of the Holy Spirit needed to reckon with the Spirit both as a person sent by God and also a person who is God, rather than an 'emission of some divine force detachable from God ...'[3] It was the argument made, for example, by the Cappadocian Fathers – Basil, Bishop of Caesarea; Gregory, Bishop of Nyssa; and Gregory Nazianzus, Archbishop of Constantinople – and the Cypriate Metropolitan Bishop, Epiphanius of Salamis. Drawing on the work of such theologians, the Council concluded that the Holy Spirit may be understood only in relation to the specific works the Spirit undertakes within the Triune God's economy. Thus the third article of the Creed holds identity and action together, describing who the Spirit is (proceeding from the Father and the Son, with whom he is to be worshipped and glorified), and what the Spirit does as the One who speaks through Scripture (the prophets), is the principal agent in baptism, gathers and forms the Church, enables forgiveness, and kindles future-facing hope within the hearts of disciples. It is only in this experience of the Spirit's work, and in knowing such work to be the extension and fulfilment of Christ's work, that the earliest Christians could give voice to a doctrine of the Holy Spirit and to a coherent doctrine of God.

## Jesus and the Holy Spirit

Throughout the New Testament, the Holy Spirit is interwoven with the work of Jesus. In response to Mary's question about the possibility of her conceiving a holy son, Gabriel replied, 'the Holy Spirit will come upon you, and the power of the Most High will overshadow you' (Luke 1.35). The boy to be born would be God's by some miracle of the Holy Spirit. Later, at his baptism, the voice from heaven affirming Jesus' identity and commending him to those who would listen was accompanied by the Spirit of God in the form of a dove – symbol of the presence and anointing of the Holy Spirit (Mark 1.10; Matt. 3.16; Luke 3.22). The scene is often regarded as a trinitarian vignette, showing the interrelated work of the three persons but also indicating something of the eternal mutuality within the Godhead. Immediately after it, Jesus went out into the desert to do spiritual battle with the devil's temptations, suggesting that the anointing of the Spirit enabled him to do that work. That this is also the beginning of Jesus' ministry emphasizes the extent to which Christ lived pneumatically, i.e. in the power and under the influence of the Holy Spirit.

Of all four gospels, the picture of Jesus and his disciples we encounter in John's gospel is the most overtly and directly pneumatological. Throughout John emphasizes the necessity of the Holy Spirit for those who would be followers of Christ. For example, in his encounter with Nicodemus, Jesus told his night-time visitor, 'no-one can enter the Kingdom of God without being born of water and the Spirit' (John 3.5–8). Later in the narrative, Jesus explained to the disciples that though he would be leaving they would not be without him because the Holy Spirit would be with them:

> I will ask the Father and he will send you another Advocate to be with you forever. This is the Spirit of Truth whom the world cannot receive because it neither sees him nor knows him. You know him because he abides with you and he will

be in you … the Advocate, the Holy Spirit, whom the Father will send will teach you everything and remind you of all that I have said to you. (John 14.15–26)

When the Advocate comes, whom I will send to you from the Father, the Spirit of truth whom comes from the Father, he will testify on my behalf. (John 15.26)

If I do not go away, the Advocate will not come to you: but if I go, I will send him to you. And when he comes he will prove the world wrong about sin and righteousness and judgement … (John 16.7–8)

The Greek adjective *parakletos* which is translated *advocate* has its substantive meaning in the court of law, equivalent to the Latin *advocatus*, meaning someone who is called to help or support a case for the defence. It is sometimes translated *comforter*, mirroring the work done by an advocate in offering strength and support to one's argument in court by bearing witness of behalf of another (*comforter* is a compound word made up of two Latin words, *cum fortis*, meaning to add strength). Throughout the Johannine material it is usually applied to the Holy Spirit (with the exception of 1 John 2.1, where it is applied to Jesus), but the description given here in chapters 14–16 is interesting because the work of the Holy Spirit is identical to the work of the Christ described in the same gospel. For example, the Holy Spirit is within the disciples just like Jesus (compare 14.17 with 14.20); the Holy Spirit is their teacher (compare 14.26 with 13.13); the Holy Spirit gives testimony and bears witness (compare 15.26 with 8.14).[4] The point is to demonstrate that Jesus and the Holy Spirit are of a piece with each other; the Spirit continues Christ's work within them and alongside them and through them. As if to drive the point home, John described how the resurrected Jesus appeared to the disciples and commissioned them, 'as the Father has sent me, so I am sending you' before giving them the gift of the Holy Spirit, 'he breathed on them and said to them, "receive the Holy Spirit ..."' (John 20.21–22). For those who wanted to remain friends and disciples of Christ, obediently following his teaching and living in the light of his resurrection, the gift of the Holy Spirit, the Advocate, was necessary. And that this gift was so close to the giver as to almost be identical with Christ mattered; this Spirit would not simply remind them of the things Christ taught, but he would direct them to Christ.

Perhaps that is why at Pentecost when Peter stood up to preach, he pointed not to the miraculous and sudden coming of the gift-giving Spirit but to the one to whom the Spirit drew their attention: 'Jesus of Nazareth, a man of wonders attested to you by God with deeds of power, wonders, and signs that God did through him among you ... whom you crucified and killed ... but God raised him up ... Being, therefore, exalted at the right of God ... he poured out this that you both see and hear' (Acts 2.22–33). The spiritual birth of the Church, and the miraculous coming of the Holy Spirit in tongues of fire and the sound of a rushing wind, was the work of the resurrected and ascended Christ. The Spirit, therefore, is self-effacing and Christocentric.[5] The earliest theologians of the Church argued that this is necessary in God's economy because it is the Son only, who, by the incarnation, holds the image of the invisible God before human beings (Col. 1.15) and is the one in whom and through whom those same human beings may participate in the life of God. He is thus the only one of whom it may be said, *'he is homoousios with the Father, and homoousios with human beings'* and that this is the predicate of our knowledge of God.[6] This being the case, 'the Holy Spirit does not bring to Christians any independent knowledge of God, or add any new content to God's self-revelation' but instead he comes to make real and present to us the revelation of God in Christ.[7]

## The Holy Spirit and Christians

But not only does understanding the Spirit help us to understand Christ and *vice versa*; understanding the person and work of the Spirit helps us to make sense of the Church, which is Christ's body. The Spirit is the gatherer of the Church, the principal agent in the dominical sacraments of baptism and Holy Communion, and one who enables Christians to live as disciples of Jesus Christ.

St Paul, for example, explained the pneumatological nature of the Church in Galatians 4 and later in Romans 8 using the idea of *adoption*. Though an unusual practice in first-century Judaism, it was common in wider contemporary culture and allowed him to explain how it is that Christians share in Christ's inheritance as Son of the Father. In the context of a discussion of salvation, God 'sending his own Son in the likeness of sinful flesh that the just requirement of the law may be fulfilled' (Rom. 8.3) and the perfecting work of the Spirit for 'those who set their minds on things of the Spirit' (Rom. 8.5), he argued that,

> if by the Spirit you put to death the deeds of the body, you will live. For all who are led by the Spirit of God are children of God ... for you have received a spirit of adoption. When we cry 'Abba! Father!' it is that very Spirit bearing witness with our spirit that we are children of God. (Rom. 8.13–16)

There are consistencies here with his earlier letter to the Galatians,

> God sent his son ... so that we might receive adoption as children. And because you are children, God has sent the Spirit of his Son into our hearts, crying 'Abba! Father!' So you are no longer a slave but a child, and if a child then an heir through God. (Gal. 4.4–7)

Adopted children are brought into the family and given a place and status that is exactly that of a son or daughter. It would be tempting to see this metaphor as conveying something about the relationship between God and the Church, or much worse, God and individual believers (sons and daughters of God). But that's not St Paul's intention. It is first about the relationship of Christians to their older brother, Jesus Christ, and only then between Christians and God the Father. This is precisely because Jesus reveals what it is to be a son of the Father, and so without him we could not know what it means to be a child of God. But, to complicate matters a little, lest we fall into the trap of thinking God has multiple sons and daughters of which Christ is an archetypal example, St Paul argued elsewhere that only in Christ is adoption real and meaningful. Thus through the sacrament of baptism are Christians buried with Christ to be raised with Christ, and thus *share* in Christ's resurrection life as heirs to the promises made to him by the Father (Rom. 6.5–11).[8] A bigger and more profound incarnational theology is at work here than might have initially been thought: salvation is not enacted between God and human creatures *per se*, but between God the Father and a single human creature, Jesus Christ, God's Son, and then through the Spirit to all who are one with him.

Adoptees participate in Christ's status, and are thus filled with the Spirit of Christ (the Son), liberated by Christ, and destined to inherit with Christ. Adoptees are not sons and daughter in their own right, existing somehow alongside Christ; rather, adoptees share in Christ's sonship. Hence it is that by the Spirit of *Christ* that Christians also call God, 'Abba! Father!' These are Christ's words first, and then may they be spoken by his Church: he called God his father, and those who are one with him may do the same (e.g. Matt. 11.27; Luke 10.21–22; John 14.9).[9]

But adoption is not only about status. Like much of the apostle's thinking, the indicative theological presentation has moral implications attached to it. Those who are adopted in the Spirit endeavour to live as children of God, and thus, according to Cranfield, 'seek wholeheartedly to be and think and say and do that which is pleasing to Him …'[10] St Paul made the point clearly when he picked up the theme of the Holy Spirit in Galatians 5, building on the foundation laid in 4.4–7. He instructed his readers, 'walk by the Spirit, and do not gratify the desires of the flesh … those who belong to Christ Jesus have crucified the flesh ... Live by the Spirit, and let us also be guided by the Spirit' (Gal. 5.16-25). As Bruce summarizes it, 'walk by the Spirit' means 'let your conduct be directed by the Spirit.'[11] Making sense of this is not easy.

At first reading, it might sound as though the pathway to bearing good fruit is to be vigilant about avoiding sin, such that the paragraph is built upon a negative command, 'do not gratify the flesh'. Hence the list of 'the works of the flesh' in verses 19–21. But in effect this means reading the sentence backwards, 'do not gratify the flesh and you will live by the Spirit' becomes 'do not do these things listed in verses 19–21, and you will live by the Spirit'. There are, of course, plenty of approaches to moral discernment that take this view: knowing what not to do leaves much scope for what may be done. But that makes ethical discourse a less constructive discipline than it ought to be in our contemporary culture, where so much happens in the world that scripture and tradition do not comment about. On closer inspection – and if we read the sentence forwards – this paragraph is actually more positive and constructive. It is, in fact, a promise, 'walk by the Spirit and you will not gratify the flesh'. St Paul's concern is not with sin but with the Spirit. He thinks the Holy Spirit is a trustworthy guide. As such Christians do not need to self-analyse their sinfulness but to be attentive to the Holy Spirit. The textual evidence for this rests on a technical point about the aorist subjunctive used in v. 16b, *kai epithumian sarkos ou me teleste*, the best rendering of which is something like, 'and you will not fulfil the desires of the flesh'. The imperative is, therefore, not about Christian avoidance of sin, but Christian attentiveness to the Holy Spirit. As such, the two parts of v. 16 should be read alongside one another (paratactically), 'walk by the Spirit' (imperative), 'and you will not gratify the desires of the flesh' (promise) rather than as a subordinate clause. In reading it this way the tone shifts from a burdensome task to a liberating opportunity: attentiveness to the Spirit will always render good fruit. This is the practical substance of the Christian discernment.

\*\*\*\*\*

If the Holy Spirit is central to our understanding of the Christian life, how then are we to keep in step with the Spirit? In other words, how does the Spirit work in our discerning and deliberating over ethical decisions? How should Christians engage with the Spirit in the process of thinking towards the best course of action? Answering such questions seems key to an integrated ethics of discipleship, where, as we have seen, the Christian life is a Spirit-filled one. Certainly, as described above, both Jesus and St Paul thought that the Spirit would offer leadership and guidance (John 16.13, Gal. 5.25). But admitting to seeking divine guidance about moral decisions is not the same as getting a direct answer, and it can be greeted with some suspicion by onlookers – consider the treatment of Prime Minister Tony Blair when he admitted to praying about political decisions.[12] Even when Christians do pray and discern together, they may not agree on the course of action (though that does not prevent prayer being weaponized in disagreement or debate). Deliberation is necessary, and the lead of the Holy Spirit is essential, but human agents must also take responsibility for the decisions and actions that follow from them; turning to the Holy Spirit's lead is not an abdication of agency or responsibility precisely because it requires the discipline of discernment rooted in humility and obedience.

I began this chapter by looking back to the hopeful context in which Christians exist as those awaiting the coming of Christ. To enable Christians to wait meaningfully, the Spirit is given to lead and to guide. In this section I will consider what shape discernment must take, before then considering how prayer and contemplation might play a role in ethical deliberation.

## The Spirit and Moral Discernment

In a masterful essay on the topic of ethical discernment,[13] Rowan Williams has argued that Christian decision-making is shaped by the relational matrix between God, Church and creation that is definitive of Christian existence. Relationship is basic and foundational for all human being, but especially for Christian anthropologies where questions of identity, meaning and purpose are all considered in relation to Christ. Williams argues that with this in mind a Christian approach to decision-making will always seek to ensure that the actions that follow 'show the character of the God ... in such a way that my actions become something given into the life of the community in such a way that what results is glory – the radiating, the visibility, of God's beauty in the world'.[14] They make sense within the community, and they show forth something of God to the community. My actions are not simply my own if I am a Christian, because I am part of a body of believers, conjoined through Christ the head (cf. 1 Cor. 12.12–27). My decisions and actions take place in this communal context. In emphasizing the interplay between community and God, Williams opens up possibilities for thinking about the role of the Spirit in moral discernment.

One way to treat the passages discussed above from Galatians and Romans is as a defence of an entirely subjective approach to Christian ethics: the Spirit leads *me*, and will guide *me*, and teach *me*. After all, the Spirit has been given to *me* as well as to *us*. But that fails to acknowledge that St Paul wrote to communities of people, gathered around Christ, who shared life together (Acts 2.43–47). They were communities with common bonds through baptism, and common focus in prayer and worship. It was to the community that he said, 'be guided by the Spirit' (Gal. 5.25). Thus, it is to the Spirit at work in the community that Christians must attend, rather than simply any fresh revelation the self-same Spirit might offer them individually. So doing prevents our arrogance and pride

if another Christian comes to a different conclusion and decides in different ways from myself, and if I can still recognize their discipline and practice as sufficiently like mine to sustain a conversation, this leaves my own decisions to some extent under question.[15]

Keeping the posture of openness to the Spirit, discussed in the previous chapter, means staying alert to dissenting voices within the Christian community, lest those in control perceive that only they know the mind of Christ. It means being slow to reject the faith of another because they do not conform to our own views, while also holding to our convictions. It means ensuring that the means of spiritual discernment are communal and corporate, not individual and singular. It requires personal humility – being prepared to think again, to repent, and to think with others.

But more than that, it means acknowledging that the Spirit always works in and through the whole community. As Volker Rabens has argued, the communal and relational aspect of the pneumatic community is the most significant for St Paul's understanding of growth in discipleship and holiness, as it is through the dispersed gifts of the Spirit that the whole people is built up in common life and faith.[16] Take, for example, the body-ecclesiology of 1 Cor. 12 where the apostle states: 'to each is given the manifestation of the Spirit for the common good'. Or take the later Pauline theology of Ephesians, where the gifts of the Spirit are '... to equip the saints for the work of ministry, for building up the body of Christ, until all of us come to the unity of faith and the knowledge of the Son of God' (Eph. 4.11– 13). The leading and guiding of the Spirit must not be separated from this ordinary work of the Spirit in the life of the whole Church. That is to say, there is no biblical warrant to think of ethical discernment and the leading of the Holy Spirit as a distinct category of work which the Spirit does in the Church, and thus something that is more subjective and personal than corporate and ecclesial.

If the Spirit is given to the whole community to make us Christians who are well equipped to live between the resurrection and the *parousia*, then attending to the Holy Spirit's leadership and guidance is something that must be done by the whole Church. The mode of that discernment is prayer, to which I now turn, drawing upon the work of Karl Barth as a guide.

## Prayer and Christian Ethics

In the paragraphs of the *Church Dogmatics*, which occupied Karl Barth's final days, he took as his theme *The Christian Life*.[17] In it he argued that the heart of the project of Christian ethics is prayer, understood paradigmatically through the lens of the Lord's Prayer.[18] Barth argued that prayer is the 'lifelong invocation of God', calling upon God as father in much the same way that St Paul advocated in the epistles to the Galatians and Romans.[19] The end of such invocation is intimacy and relationship, pursuit of God for God's own sake, in response to the grace shown in Jesus Christ. The realization of the freedom to pray to this God in this way is a work of the Holy Spirit, who 'discloses … impels … and empowers' Christians to do so.[20] This is surely what St Paul meant when he says 'we do not know how to pray as we ought, but that very Spirit intercedes with sighs too deep for words'. (Rom. 8.26).[21] The guarantee that this way of life is necessary and good is that, in much the same way as the dominical sacraments, Jesus Christ commanded and taught that his disciples pray in exactly that way. Barth argued,

> by the power of the Holy Spirit he is here and now the living Lord of his community, of Christians … and there thus arises for all who recognize and acknowledge him as their Lord the obligatory command – the first of all commands – that they do as he does and join with him in calling upon God the Father.[22]

To pray, then, is to live consciously in the presence of Jesus Christ, attentive to the Holy Spirit who makes Christ present to us through scripture (where we hear Christ's command to 'pray like this', cf. Matt. 6.9), and through the sacraments of baptism and the Eucharist (where Christians are enlivened and nourished by Christ, cf. Rom. 6.5–11 and 1 Cor. 11.24–25). It is to punctuate each day, week, month and year with specific moments of prayer and intercession, and to frame and perceive the day's other tasks through the lens of God's will. To pray is to *follow* Christ in directing our lives to God, praying Christ's prayer (the Lord's Prayer) with him. In this sense, prayer is about orientation; it disrupts any hint of self-obsession or self-interest as through it Christians genuinely attend to the Father. Such an account even disrupts the idea that prayer is about self-expression, since to pray with Christ is to pray liturgically – following the pattern established by him. It is also about participation. Christ is the only mediator between human creatures and God the Father (John 14.6) and thus the only one through whom our prayers may be truthful and accurate. So it is that, theologically speaking, praying with Christ is necessary if we are to really pray at all. The Spirit of Christ is given to teach and train Christians to pray.

If it was simply about orientation Christ would be reduced to a mere example of human spirituality. So, Barth argued, precisely because the Holy Spirit makes Christ present to us, and that with Christ we may invoke God in prayer and call upon the Father for help and guidance, the act of invocation is itself an event that takes place between two people – the Holy Spirit of God and the praying Christian. As Christians pray, therefore, they may expect to be aware of God through 'experience, perception, contemplation and resolve'. In other words, prayer of this kind changes the pray-er by bringing her into contact with God:

> In the Holy Spirit, God presents and attests himself to the not at all holy spirits of these people in such a way that within the limits of their spirits, and despite the very painful nature of these limits, they are summoned and raised up for experience, perception, and understanding, for free and freely active acceptance of what he was and is and will be for the world, of what he ... has done and does and will for do all men, and therefore for them too ...[23]

Where the praying Christian is attentive to Jesus Christ, made present by the Holy Spirit, and prays with Christ to the Father, then she is made more open and aware of God's will and more ready and willing to endorse it both for herself and for the world around. And others around her, also prayerfully attentive to Christ, will attest and affirm her discernment. Praying Christians are able to make sense of what has been, to see more clearly the present, and step towards the future with boldness and confidence in God.[24] The practical substance of Christian life, what it is that disciples of Jesus decide and do, is known only as this attentiveness to God takes place.

This last point is unusual in Christian ethical discourse. It is much more common to discuss and debate key texts, authorities and traditions than it is to pray together for wisdom and guidance. But, again, like St Paul, Barth addresses a Christian community in which prayer and worship, sacraments and Bible study, are core activities through which faith is nurtured and the people are held together by the Spirit of Christ.[25] And, like the apostle, he expects that what happens in those 'religious' events will impact the whole lived existence of the Church. This is so, not because the Christians are especially holy or good, but because God guarantees it through the Holy Spirit. In this context, prayer is not a subjective or private means of getting special or esoteric knowledge; prayer is the whole Church's pneumatic work: 'it is the Church ... who ... call upon God ...'.[26] And therefore, we might add, through the Holy Spirit, the Church who encounters God and the Church who grows into obedience of God's will.

## Summary

To describe the Holy Spirit as *Lord and Giver of Life* is to express the fact that all real human life is only possible when enlivened by God. In this time of waiting for Christ's return and living in the light of the resurrection, the Church is the community of the Spirit in which the will of God is pursued and discerned

FAITHFUL LIVING

through prayerful attentiveness to Jesus Christ. To live this way is to trust the indicative truth that Christians have new life in Christ because they have died with him (Rom. 6.5) and therefore crucified the flesh (Gal. 5.24), and have now been raised with him (Col. 3.1). It is also to take seriously the place of prayer as communion with God, and thus as place of radical encounter and transformation. If ethics necessarily involves deciding and acting out of our identity, then for Christians prayer is central to ethical deliberation precisely because we most fully know who we are in proximity to Jesus Christ.

## Questions

Do you ever pray before making decisions?

When you pray, do you expect an answer? Do you ask others to pray, and do they expect the same?

How do you discern the Holy Spirit's guidance?

## Further reading

Fee, Gordon, *God's Empowering Presence: The Holy Spirit in the Letters of Paul* (Peabody, MA: Hendrickson Publishing, 1994).

### Notes

1 Gordon Fee, *God's Empowering Presence: The Holy Spirit in the Letters of Paul* (Peabody, MA: Hendrickson Publishing, 1994), 876.

2 The theme of Christ's presence in ethical decision-making is taken up by Christopher R.J. Holmes, *Ethics in the Presence of Christ* (London: T&T Clark/Bloomsbury, 2012).

3 T.F. Torrance, *The Trinitarian Faith* (Edinburgh: T&T Clark, 1988), 192.

4 For more on the use of the preposition 'in' within John's gospel see, Andreas Köstenberger, *Encountering John: The Gospel in Historical, Literary, and Theological Perspective* (Grand Rapids: Baker Academic, 1999), 154–5.

5 Anthony Thiselton describes the work of the Spirit in Scripture as 'Christ-

centred' in his comprehensive study *The Holy Spirit: In Biblical Teaching, Through the Centuries, and Today* (London: SPCK, 2013), 70–1.

6 Christopher Holmes makes the same point more sharply when he says, 'the Son – and only the Son – is sent for us' in his *The Holy Spirit*, New Studies in Dogmatics Series (Grand Rapids: Zondervan, 2015), 206.

7 Torrance, *Trinitarian Faith*, 203.

8 On the connection between baptism and ethics, see Vigen Guroian, 'The Gift of the Holy Spirit: Reflections on Baptism and Growth in Holiness' in *Studies in Christian Ethics* Vol. 12.1 (1999), 23–34.

9 It is worth noting here that, since Paul had never been to Rome when he wrote the letter, that the phrase 'Abba! Father!' was known to them and thus scholars assume it was an early Christian acclamation deriving from Christ's own piety. See F.F. Bruce, *The Epistle to the Galatians*, The New International Greek Testament Commentary (Grand Rapids: Eerdmans, 1982), 199. For commentary on the probable liturgical setting of the 'Abba!' cry, see Fee, *Empowering Presence*, 409.

10 Cranfield, *Romans*, 393.

11 Bruce, *Galatians*, 243. Christopher Holmes' discussion of the same paragraph is a helpful addition to Bruce's commentary. Holmes argues that St Paul's argument summarizes a kind of competition between what is real and what is not real, such that only those who live in the light of the Spirit live in the new creation (6.15), but the old creation no longer exists (2 Cor. 5.17). See his essay, 'The Perfecting God' in Eilers and Strobel, *Sanctified by Grace*, 75–88.

12 Tony Blair discussed this in an interview with Michael Parkinson on the ITV1 show, *Parkinson*, broadcast on 4 March 2006. (See http://news.bbc.co.uk/1/hi/4772142.stm accessed November 2018.)

13 Rowan Williams, 'Making Moral Decisions', in Robin Gill (ed.), *The Cambridge Companion to Christian Ethics* (Cambridge: Cambridge University Press, 2001), 4–15.

14 Williams, 'Making Moral Decisions', 6–7.

15 Williams, 'Making Moral Decisions', 11.

16 Volker Rabens, *The Holy Spirit and Ethics in Paul: Transformation and Empowering for Religious-Ethical Life* (Augsburg: Fortress Press, 2014), ch. 6.

17 Karl Barth, *The Christian Life: Church Dogmatics IV/4 Lecture Fragments*, trans. Geoffrey Bromiley (Edinburgh: T&T Clark, 1981), hereafter *CD IV/4*. Barth died before completing this volume, and short of the projected five volumes of the *Church Dogmatics*.

18 The structure of these fragmentary lectures is interesting and important: the intention was for an introduction, §74, followed by a discourse on baptism, §75, and then a substantial middle section on the Lord's Prayer, §§76–8, with a final discourse on the Lord's Supper, §79. As it is, only §§74–78 exist in draft format, and only §75 was published in Barth's lifetime: Karl Barth, *CD IV/4 The Christian Life (Fragments): Baptism as the Foundation of the Christian Life* (Edinburgh: T&T Clark, 1969).

19 Barth, *CD IV/4*, 49–50. By far the best introduction to Barth's

understanding of prayer is Ashley Cocksworth, *Karl Barth on Prayer* (London: Bloomsbury/T&T Clark, 2015).

20 Barth, *CD IV/4*, 52.

21 Jean Calvin made the same point at length when he described 'the prompting of the Spirit empowering Christians to compose prayers' in his *Institutes of the Christian Religion* Vol. 2, ed. John McNeill (Philadelphia: Westminster Press, 1960), 856.

22 Barth, *CD IV/4*, 64.

23 Barth, *CD IV/4*, 90.

24 In an earlier set of lectures on the same topic published as *The Holy Spirit and the Christian Life: The Theological Basis of Ethics* (Louisville: Westminster John Knox, 1993), Barth put more emphasis on the place of conscience than he did in the *CD IV/4* fragments. He described it as a form of 'co-knowledge' of the Father's will which comes by the present work on the Holy Spirit among Christian believers, 65.

25 See, for example, Barth's discussion in *CD IV/4*, 133.

26 Barth, *CD IV/4*, 153.

# 9

# 'Communion of Saints, and Forgiveness of Sins': The Church and Practical Catechesis

Thus far I have suggested some examples of ethical reasoning that might be inferred from the Nicene Creed to answer the question: what kinds of lifestyle choices, decisions and actions might be implied for contemporary disciples by the theological substance of the Christian faith? I have also sketched the moral terrain in relation to the eschaton, and the spiritual disciplines that are necessary to keep in step with the Holy Spirit. The goal has been a co-inherent and integrated approach to the Christian life, connecting the sorts of theological material with which many Christians are familiar through liturgy and worship to the concrete circumstances of human life. In this final chapter I turn to an important constituency within this conversation – local church leaders or pastors. Local churches are communities of saints and sinners, in which the faithful must learn to inhabit their identities as people revived in resurrection power by the Holy Spirit while also wrestling with the realities of brokenness and sin, discernment and decision-making. Church is a place of communion, of coming together around Jesus Christ, and of sharing life. But precisely because those who gather are human beings dogged by sin and awaiting the eschaton, Church is a place where forgiveness must be received and given. It must be received from God in Christ, and received from fellow disciples. It must also be given to fellow disciples. This giving and receiving is part of the dynamic of learning to follow Christ.

But more than the social reality of learning, an integrated ethics of discipleship must first reckon with the local church because it must be meaningful to all disciples and that means to the vast majority of Christians who are not members of the academy or theologically educated church officials. Pastors have responsibility for what happens in local church contexts, and who navigate the reality of the communion of forgiven sinner-saints. Second, if it is to be an *integrated* ethics of discipleship, it must not only resist the urge to fragment the Christian life into beliefs and practices but the urge to disentangle the supposed sacred from the secular must also be resisted. The Church is made up of those who are simultaneously sinners and saints. This means reconfiguring the *whole* of life as discipleship, and this kind of vision needs resourcing if it is to be liveable.

## Thinking Catechetically

To that end, I propose an expanded notion of *catechesis* in the local church. It captures both the fragility of the context where the forgiveness of sins must be practiced often, and the possibilities afforded by the communion of saints. Catechesis has traditionally named the process of teaching the theological substance of the Christian faith. It has taken the form of a series of questions and answers to be memorized and recited in preparation for baptism or as instruction towards confirmation. The goal is to learn the basics of Christianity. The syllabus often included memorizing key passages of Scripture, the Apostles' Creed and the Lord's Prayer before reciting them in public prior to baptism (or, in the case of infant baptism, the Godparents would recite them). Because of this, it has been most associated with initiation in local churches and given quite a rudimentary status within the tradition. A bit like a driving theory test, it's what you have to pass through in order to become a full member. In one parish where I was vicar, a potential confirmand who had come to faith late in life refused to attend what the PCC had named 'Confirmation Catechesis' because he associated the word 'catechesis' with what he remembered from his schooldays. (We eventually changed the name of the preparation.) But, despite the potential for infantilism, the connection between instruction and initiation has biblical roots.

When Jesus gave the Great Commission, he told his followers to 'make disciples of all nations; baptize and teach them all that I have taught you' (Matt. 28.19).[1] Here teaching in the context of baptism is part of the convert's initiation into the life of faith. In the early Church the process of becoming a member could take up to two years from expressing initial interest in Christianity right through to full admission at baptism. And evidence from the fourth century suggests that baptisms tended to take place only once per year, at Easter, to connect the liturgical worship directly to that which it symbolized – the death and resurrection of new believers with Christ (see Rom. 6.1–11).[2] Catechism therefore took several months, even years, before completion. In some cases it was divided into two parts: the period leading up to baptism, where the emphasis was on learning the liturgical calendar, absorbing apostolic teaching, and reading Scripture; and then subsequently after Easter, where the emphasis was on eucharistic theology and practice. Catechesis came to be associated, therefore, with learning the basics, laying doctrinal foundations, and enabling the catechumens to participate as fully as possible in the worshipping life of the Church.

## Teaching in Wider New Testament Perspective

In the New Testament, teaching is much more diverse than this reading of the Great Commission might suggest. Practices of teaching and instruction go well beyond initiation. Take, for example, Acts 2.41–42, 'so those who welcomed this message were baptized, and that day about three thousand were added. They devoted themselves to the apostles' teaching and fellowship, to the breaking of bread and the prayers.' The text links teaching and instruction to conversion and baptism in the life of this fledgling congregation, but it is also clear that apostolic teaching was part of the ongoing sacramental and liturgical practices of the community as it grew and developed. The Church was *devoted* to the apostles' teaching along with worship and fellowship. According to some biblical scholars, 'devotion' here signifies an ongoing and consistent pattern, rather than a one-off or seasonal fixation.[3] Just as we cannot imagine that the early Church ever moved beyond its regular celebration of the Eucharist or grew out of prayer, so too we cannot imagine a Church that was not committed to the rehearsal of authoritative teaching.

Apostolic teaching was the community's benchmark for its life together. For example, when St Paul exhorted the Roman Christians to remain faithful and avoid people who would lead them astray, the apostles' teaching was in view: 'I urge you, brothers and sisters, to keep an eye on those who cause dissensions and offences in opposition to the teaching that you have learned; avoid them. For such people do not serve our Lord Jesus Christ' (Rom. 16.17). In discerning the appointment of overseers and bishops, the candidate's faithfulness to the apostolic teaching was regarded as a sign of their worthiness for the role: 'for a bishop … must have a firm grasp of the word that is trustworthy in accordance with the teaching, so that he may be able to preach with sound doctrine and refute those who contradict it' (Titus 1.7–9). And the ongoing health of the congregations depended upon their willingness to rehearse the apostolic teaching for one another's benefit: 'let the word of Christ dwell in you richly; teach and admonish one another in all wisdom; and with gratitude in your heart sing psalms, hymns, and spiritual songs to God' (Col. 3.16). Indeed, the office of teacher was a recognized gift to enable the ongoing health of the Church, 'to equip the saints for the work of ministry, for building up the body of Christ' (Eph. 4.11–16). This kind of teaching may seem quite different from catechesis as we commonly understand the idea, but I suggest that it is *catechetical* precisely because it is focused on the foundational teachings of the apostles. Disciples do not leave their foundations behind, as if baptism were only something of the past and not the future also (cf. Rom. 6.4), and therefore they do not leave behind the apostolic teaching associated with it. To borrow a metaphor, catechesis lays theological foundations to build the Christian life upon. The ongoing challenge for local church leaders is to enable God's people to make sense of the foundations so as to construct something appropriate and consistent on them; there's no use building a skyscraper on foundations made for a two-story house – it will fall down. Foundations make a difference to what is possible. The theologian Richard Osmer describes the task facing the local church as follows:

> It must be a place where Scripture and theology are taught in such a manner that they become an important part of the interpretive framework that persons used to make sense of their lives and the surrounding world. Theology must not be remote from everyday life but must imbue it with a deeper and richer meaning as the arena in which persons live out their vocations before God.[4]

Osmer's vision is compelling precisely because it steps towards the challenge of discipleship, namely integrating belief and practice. Congregations that are hampered by the notion that theology and Scripture are for Church, and offer no resource for living well, will find that their spiritual health suffers – they'll be fragmented. Healthy churches are those where people are enabled to connect with faith with their everyday lives in meaningful ways.[5] Osmer's solution to the problem is in good teaching that deliberately sets out to make those connections. I agree with him, and moreover, I suggest that the teaching he describes is actually akin to the New Testament approach, in which the foundational theological ideas about Christ are rehearsed and revisited as resources to live by. As such, a catechesis that supports an integrated ethics of discipleship must be more than an adult-education class or a modern version of the question-answer syllabus. In what follows I have not produced a policy document to make my point but an outline of the key ingredients that are necessary to do the work. I have called it a proto-manifesto. This chapter is meant to be constructive not critical. I write as a parish priest, having served in licensed ministry in a variety of contexts over the past 15 years. As a fellow pastor I am convinced that the local church community is the most effective context in which to address the formation of Christian disciples and through which to enable an integrated Christian life. Recovering this sense of purpose matters for the future health and ongoing mission of the Church.

## Towards a Catechesis for an Integrated Ethics of Discipleship

My proposal is intentionally modest. I am deliberately avoiding a fixed model for catechesis because each context in which such catechesis will happen will be different. Rather, I am focusing on what I take to be the three key ingredients of a whole-life adult catechesis, what I am calling three 'modes of thinking' that can help pastors, priests, ministers and leaders with the task. These will need to be instantiated in different ways depending on context and may be held together in creative tension. The modes are liturgical thinking, pedagogical thinking, and responsive thinking.

### *Think Liturgically*

To think liturgically is to think inter-connectedly, bringing the whole of who we are into the purview of worship and orientating our entire lives towards Jesus Christ so that liturgy can resource faithful living.[6] Such thinking is the work of liturgical theology, 'giving a theological basis to the explanation of worship and the whole liturgical tradition of the Church'.[7] It explores the structures and movement entailed in worship, and how understanding them helps Christians to hold the whole of life before God in the moment of gathering. Liturgical theology refuses 'the reduction of liturgy to its "cultic" categories' (those ritual experiences that elevate the hearts of those who love liturgy or raise the hackles of those who do not): it focuses on liturgy as '*leitourgia* – a ministry or calling to act in this world after the fashion of Christ …'.[8] Broadly speaking, liturgy concerns itself with purposeful attention to the gospel in gathered worship, by close attention to Scripture and by enacting the movement of the people towards God in Christ. It is about shape and direction. Where we think of liturgy simply as orders of service or scripts we do not do justice to the *leitourgia* and we forget that 'a liturgical text exists not for its own sake but for the sake of enactment'.[9] It is to be prayed, enacted and lived. Liturgical theology works in the interplay between the particularity of gathered worship and the universality of life lived elsewhere. It 'works' in this sense by marking time on a daily, weekly, seasonal and yearly basis. It names seasons in direct relation to the gospel narrative, puncturing any inflated claim we may make on our own existence by reminding us that we are creatures. Liturgical theology thus (re-)focuses our attention on God to help us to make sense of ourselves.[10] It is patterned and habitual: instructing Christians in their identity as disciples by repeatedly hearing and responding to the gospel. Scripted liturgy is thus about the discipline of worship – redirecting piety from any experiential narcissism or arguments about preference.[11]

One way in which the Church has maintained this Godward focus is its shared calendar of festivals, revolving elliptically around Christmas and Easter, seeking to encourage faithfulness by rehearsing Scripture. Inhabiting Scripture's witness to Christ from Advent to the Feast of Christ the King is learning to

inhabit the gospel, to journey with those who long for God to answer his promises and to articulate our own longing (Advent);

be startled by and thankful for the unlikely ways in which God works for our good with the shepherds, foreign astrologers and the Holy Family, and to ask for grace to see what the Lord is doing (Christmas and Epiphany);

feel the relief at many long years of prayer answered with Simeon and Anna, and to find courage to keep going while we too wait for God to answer us (Candlemas);

rid ourselves of those distractions that so easily hinder our growth in faith and to be reminded again of what matters most (Lent);

journey with our Lord Jesus through Holy Week, and in so doing see the truth about ourselves and our world within his suffering and death (Holy Week);

be, once again, startled by the miraculous power and overwhelming graciousness of the resurrection, to know that death does not have the final word because that belongs to Jesus Christ who is risen from the dead and therefore speaks hope and love to a world of brokenness and pain (Easter);

receive the life-giving gift of the Spirit to connect us with Christ and thus enable us to share his resurrection life so that we may in turn live it in the world (Pentecost);

read Scripture in the light of this gospel and learn from the examples of others who've gone before us so that we may stay faithful to Christ in the power of the Spirit (Saints' Days and Ordinary time);[12]

lift our eyes beyond the immediate, to see the one who will come again in glory and who is the goal of all creation (Christ the King).

The point is to make sense of the present in the light of the gospel. The calendar orientates us beyond the culture and context in which we live to the wider Christian story in which all creation co-inheres.

Liturgical gatherings are an intensive subspecies of this kind of thinking. Their intention is the unveiling of God's glory.[13] Gathering involves separation from the world[14] in order to be sent back into the world – 'Go in Peace, to love and serve the Lord' – so that we may live faithfully as disciples of Christ.[15] In between the gathering and dismissal is movement towards Christ in word and sacrament: sins are forgiven; the Scriptures are read and the gospel is preached, and the Word is heard and received; the sacrament is celebrated and Christ is pneumatically present with and within his people; the congregation is blessed to be a blessing. Liturgy thus marks space and time. It does not create places of retreat or sanctuary from the rest of life, but, rather, places of equipping and commissioning to live in the world and for the world. To live as disciples.

In terms of an integrated ethics of discipleship, thinking liturgically means regarding the worshipping life of a community as formational, constantly orientating the people to God without neglecting the world from which they've come and into which they will be sent. If successful, gathered worship impacts lifestyle choices and decisions. Thinking liturgically reframes how we engage with our own agency and the contexts in which we live and work by relativizing them to Christ and the gospel. Thinking *liturgically* about worship is a way of thinking *theologically* and *intentionally* about our lives before God; it does not mean shifting to printed orders of service with litanies and ancient prayers, but it does mean crafting public worship that claims all of life and thus resources whole-life discipleship. Thinking liturgically means thinking about the connections between the particular and the universal, the gathered and the dispersed life of the Church, and leads to worship that connects with God and thus with God's intent and purpose revealed in the gospel. Thinking liturgically enables the gathered people to come as their entire selves before God, integrating their prayer and worship with their daily round of decisions and actions. To think liturgically is to think beyond Sunday mornings, to relativize the particularity of the gathered within the whole-life worship which the New Testament requires of all disciples (Rom. 12.1–4).

## *Think Pedagogically*

To think pedagogically is to be intentional, creative and contextually appropriate in teaching the substance of the faith, so that people may learn it. Pedagogy is an academic discipline concerned with the theory and practice of teaching and learning. In practical terms, pedagogy relates to the appropriate training and qualifications of those who teach. It usually requires that those institutions that manage the learning environments will mitigate against stagnation by ensuring the ongoing professional development of its staff to respond to the various needs of students. This requires structures of growth and accountability that engage with the outcomes of a teacher's work through student feedback, monitoring assessment grades, and annual performance review. Such processes help to identify strengths and weaknesses, create resources for teacher development, and enhance overall classroom quality. Increasingly in the UK, higher education students are surveyed by institutions and national organizations such as the Office for Students at the beginning and end of their programmes to monitor the quality of an institution's delivery. For those who learn in these formal environments there is increasingly both academic and pastoral support available to help them achieve the desired outcome. Though it may sound mechanistic and administrative, the goal of such an approach is, in theory at least, to create a learning environment that enables the most meaningful learning for students.

But the study of pedagogy also involves wider metaphysical concerns which provide the bigger context wherein teaching and learning can be worked out. It frames teaching in relation to the purpose and goals of the community. Places of learning usually serve something other than themselves, and one of the tasks of pedagogy is to align contextual practice with overall purpose. The teaching and learning do not occur in a vacuum, isolated from other aspects of life. It is both contextual and purposive.

A specifically *Christian* pedagogy is distinctive because it locates the whole discourse about the purpose and practicalities of teaching and learning within a theological description of the Christian life. Disciples are learners first and foremost[16] and Christian pedagogy weaves together the 'the spiritual and moral as well as intellectual formation of students …'[17] thus reorientating the pedagogical project towards the metaphysics of the gospel. Education thus belongs within a discourse around the meaning, purpose and direction of human existence, 'to enable [people] to fulfil God's purposes for their lives centred in Christ'.[18] *Christian* pedagogy therefore pursues holistic learning. While the local church is obviously not a formal classroom of the sort you'd find in a higher education institution, it is a learning environment. Church is for holistic learning, in which 'individuals bring their whole selves … not merely the proper or "correct" self, but the one who thinks, feels and questions life, reality and relationships'.[19] And, moreover, in which the same people want their faith 'to connect with their weekday worlds …'[20] In proposing that we think pedagogically, I am saying that it is helpful to think purposefully about teaching and learning in church, and that pastors are equipped appropriately for the task. People gather to be helped to live Christianly, to think theologically, to be challenged and to grow. The goal of teaching in this context is to make connections between what is learned and understood in worship, and what is lived and experienced beyond the gatherings. The goal is whole-life discipleship.

Local churches are specific environments where 'concrete communities and individuals are given the opportunity to appropriate Christian faith in deeply particular ways'.[21] They are learning environments in which the whole gathering is viewed pedagogically – not just the sermon slot, which so readily mimics a lecture. Everything we do when gathered together has pedagogic value. But we often assume that learning will happen indirectly. Ministerial training rarely includes teaching skills (certainly there are preaching skills, but these tend to be about oration rather than pedagogy), and congregations do not come to a gathered church with the same level of preparedness to learn as those entering a classroom. Direct connections have to be made between the theology that underpins what we do when we gather, the faith we profess and the lives we lead outside of the gathering. And precisely because 'each community of faith resides within a parish, a place, a context' they will have their particular and specific needs when it comes to making these connections.[22] Though the purpose is always '... to create a context in which faith can be awakened, supported and challenged',[23] the practical nuts and bolts of teaching and learning need to adapt and flex according to the people who live there, and the history and culture that has shaped them. Those who teach need a tool kit for teaching that is more than the traditional lecture-style sermon or reading group. Teaching that appreciates learning styles, that encourages discussion, and that facilitates and develop peoples' curiosity, and that is creative and playful is increasingly important to the life of a healthy congregation. As Richard Osmer has noted,

> Understanding the culture of a congregation is a crucial part of leading that community ... The culture reflects the history of that particular community of faith, providing a language, a range of biblical and theological images, stories and concepts, and a set of social practices by which that congregation attempts to live before God. Members of the community reflect within the linguistic and conceptual parameters of this culture. Once they understand this framework ministers will be far more adept at using the material it provides to help the congregation reflect on the situations that confront it.[24]

A local congregation in the north of England situated in an urban priority area and ranked highly against the indices of multiple deprivation will likely require different pedagogical practices from one situated in the Royal Borough of Kensington and Chelsea. It will also have a very different context in which what is taught will be lived out. The goal and purpose is still discipleship, but the methods by which belief and practice are related to one another may be quite different. Indeed, the substantive theological content of the learning remains the same, but the means of teaching it will be contextual. Asking people to meet to read and discuss a commentary on the Nicene Creed will not be appropriate in a non-book culture and is more likely to undermine faith development than encourage it. Finding ways of connecting the theology of the clauses of the creed with concrete decisions faced by people on a daily basis will have a more significant effect. That's not to say people from such backgrounds should be patronized or prohibited from book-based learning, but it is to say that what is required to be successful in various contexts is *knowledge*, *understanding* and *intent*. Those with responsibility for teaching a congregation must ask both 'what material am I teaching?' and 'what is the best way to connect this material to the lives of these particular disciples of Christ?'

## *Think Responsively*

To think responsively is to organize local church life and make concrete decisions in direct response to the gospel. This is an idea that received a considerable theological attention from the theologian Karl Barth, who argued that the basic structure of the Christian life is address-response. God addresses humanity in Jesus Christ because he is God's *Word*, moving towards creation as its Lord and saviour, and seeking the welfare of creation through his sacrificial death and resurrection. But lest we think this narrative is powerful only in its ability to capture imaginations, Barth argues that the gospel also invites creatures to conformity and fulfilment of God's intended purposes. This is essentially liberating rather than limiting, since, for Barth, learning to live as God determined will actually be fulfilling. In terms of ethics, Barth summarizes the situation in one of several places by explaining that Christians are 'made responsible as we have heard the voice of the risen Lord'.[25] That it is the risen

Lord who speaks indicates that we are still thinking about the gospel and not condemnation. But that Christians are made responsible suggests that the gospel requires something of us. Jesus Christ who lives also calls his people to follow him. To be responsible is to think responsively, which is to make decisions and to act in the light of the gospel and consider what kinds of behaviours are appropriate for those who follow the resurrected Christ.

Such thinking really does require action. Considered from the perspective Barth offers, what we do has meaning: it instantiates the gospel. When thinking about an integrated ethics of discipleship and the local church catechesis that helps to enable it, the congregation and its leaders have an opportunity to respond to the gospel in concrete ways. For example, as part of its commitment to the Lordship of Jesus Christ, the local church might host a political hustings during election season to help local people understand and make sense of the claims of the rival political parties or set up a community forum to discuss local issues and act upon them; in response to the doctrine of creation, the PCC might decide to go #defaultveg for all church events, or change its electricity supplier to a renewable energy company, or offer a home group study series on our engagement with creation; in honouring the shared humanity of all people grounded in the humanity of Christ, local churches might provide disabled access, hearing loops, dyslexia friendly projection and safe spaces for people with learning difficulties; in acknowledging the reality of human suffering, local churches might stand in solidarity with the poor by feeding and clothing the homeless, or donating to charities that do.

Of course, many of these sorts of things happen in churches all of the time. But the idea is not simply to do good deeds; thinking responsively is about allowing our imaginations for what could be, and the decisions and actions we undertake, to be shaped by the gospel of Jesus Christ. It also means, therefore, cultivating dispositions of hopefulness in the light of the resurrection and prayerfulness in attention to the Holy Spirit. Hope requires imagination, because it is orientated to the future Kingdom: it looks beyond the present to what could be, anticipating Christ's rule and reign. Prayer establishes patterns of openness and attentiveness to the God of the gospel, to ensure that hope remains properly anchored and focused, undistracted by self or context. It also encourages trust; the Christian life is a response to Christ's call to follow, and does so obediently because we believe Jesus is good and his ways are good. Hopefulness and prayer motivate Christians to continue to follow when life seems hard, or the way is unclear, or the path is fraught with danger. Hope and prayer shape the horizon of Christian ethics; they are also its principal means of being alert to the gospel.

## Conclusion

If ever anyone is blessed to be a parish priest or local church pastor or minister, then they will at some point be faced with the kinds of questions with which this book has been wrestling. And this will be the case precisely because the community they'll serve, if it is really Church, will be one that is both of saints and of sinners. Such a community needs help to make sense of itself in the light of the gospel, and this work involves worship, teaching and response. The help required is not actually the work of the pastor in the first instance; it is the work the Spirit does in enlivening the scriptural witness that is summarized in the Church's Creeds. But the office of pastor, along with apostle, evangelist, prophet and teacher is also a gift of God to enable the maturity and full stature of the Church. Thus the pastor is concerned with the things the Spirit does; in Word and Sacraments, in worship and teaching, in empowering the people of God to live for Christ. The pastor thus seeks to keep in step with the Spirit. An integrated ethics of discipleship holds beliefs and actions together in faithfulness to Christ

# FAITHFUL LIVING

and in obedience to the Spirit; it treats the local church as the place of resourcing and formation to enable that work to happen. It discerns what things may be done and what actions are consistent with membership of Christ's body, the Church, through prayer and through theological inference. Such an ethic takes a willingness to learn and grow in theological understanding, but also a playfulness and openness to what believing the gospel might mean for the rest of life. It is hard work, but it is good work, and for disciples it is the only work.

## Questions

Does your worshipping life in church connect meaningfully with the rest of your life as a disciple of Christ? What's missing?

What do you think you need to enable you to respond to Christ in whole-life discipleship?

What is needed to enable the teaching office of your local church to flourish and thrive as it resources the congregation to live as integrated disciples of Christ?

## Further reading

Holmes, Christopher R. J., *Ethics in the Presence of Christ* (London: T&T Clark, 2012).
Smith, James K. A., *Desiring the Kingdom: Worship, Worldview, and Cultural Formation* (Grand Rapids: Baker Academic, 2009).

### Notes

1 The word which is here translated as 'teach' is a cognate of *didasko* rather than *katacheo* (from where we get the word catechesis) and signifies a more formal style of teaching than the oratory style associated with catechesis.
2 On the diversity and breadth of baptismal practice in the earliest centuries of the Church, see Paul Bradshaw, *The Search for the Origins of Christian Worship* (London: SPCK, 1992), ch. 7.

3 Jaroslav Pelikan, *Acts*, SCM Theological Commentary on the Bible (London: SCM Press, 2006), 58–9. See also Luke Timothy Johnson, *The Acts of the Apostles* (Collegeville, MN.: The Liturgical Press, 1992).

4 Richard Robert Osmer, *A Teachable Spirit: Recovering the Teaching Office in the Church* (Louisville: Westminster John Knox, 1990), 176.

5 See, for example, Robert Warren, *The Healthy Churches Handbook* (London: Church House Publishing, 2004). Of particular interesting is the first mark of a healthy church, one that is 'energized by faith'.

6 On liturgy and catechesis see, for example, Bryon Anderson, 'Liturgical Catechesis: Congregational Practice as Formation' in *Religious Education* Vol. 92.3 (2006), 348–62. On the formational power of liturgies see, James K. A. Smith, *Desiring the Kingdom: Worship, Worldview, and Cultural Formation* (Grand Rapids: Baker Academic, 2009).

7 Alexander Schmemann, *Introduction to Liturgical Theology* (London: The Faith Press, 1966), 14.

8 Alexander Schmemann, *For the Life of the World* (New York: St Vladimir's Press, 1973), 25.

9 Nicholas Wolterstorff, *The God We Worship: An Exploration of Liturgical Theology* (Grand Rapids: Eerdmans, 2015) 4.

10 Schmemann, *For the Life of the World*, 48–50.

11 Schmemann, *Liturgical Theology*, 22.

12 On the usefulness of ordinary time, see Craig Hovey, 'Basking and Speaking in Ordinary Time' in his *Speak Thus: Christian Language in Church and World* (Cambridge: James Clarke & Co., 2008), 129–34.

13 Thomas Cranmer, 'On Ceremonies' in *The Book of Common Prayer*.

14 Schmemann, *For the Life of the World*, 27.

15 Schmemann, *For the Life of the World*, 45.

16 See Rowan Williams, *Being Disciples: Essentials of the Christian Life* (London: SPCK, 2016), ch. 1.

17 David I. Smith and James K. A. Smith, 'Introduction: Practices, Faith, and Pedagogy' in David I. Smith and James K. A. Smith (eds.), *Teaching and Christian Practices: Reshaping Faith and Learning* (Grand Rapids: Eerdmans, 2011), 3.

18 Trevor H. Cairney, *Pedagogy and Education for Life: A Christian Reframing of Teaching, Learning, and Formation* (Eugene, OR: Cascade, 2018), 8.

19 Norma Cook Everist, *The Church as Learning Community: A Comprehensive Guide to Christian Education* (Nashville: Abingdon Press, 2002), 63.

20 Cook Everist, *The Church as Learning Community*, 167.

21 Osmer, *A Teachable Spirit*, 178.

22 Cook Everist, *The Church as Learning Community*, 21.

23 Richard Robert Osmer, *Teaching for Faith: A Guide for Teachers of Adult Classes* (Louisville: Westminster John Knox, 1992), 15.

24 Osmer, *A Teachable Spirit*, 183. On a similar point see Cairney, *Pedagogy and Education for Life*, 105–9.

25 Karl Barth, *Church Dogmatics II/2: The Doctrine of God* (Edinburgh: T&T Clark, 19), 761. For a very accessible introduction to Karl Barth's ethics see my *Doctrine in Practice: Introducing Karl Barth's Moral Theology* (Cambridge: Grove, 2016).

# Bibliography

Augustine, *Sermons 184–229Z: On the Liturgical Seasons*, trans. Edmund Hill, New York: New City Press, 1993.

Baker, David, *The Decalogue: Living as the People of God*, London: Apollos, 2017.

Balthasar, Hans Urs von, *Mysterium Paschale: The Mystery of Easter*, Edinburgh: T&T Clark, 1990.

Banner, Michael, *Christian Ethics: A Brief History*, Oxford: Wiley-Blackwell, 2009.

_____ *Christian Ethics and Contemporary Moral Problems*, Cambridge: Cambridge University Press, 1999.

_____ *The Ethics of Everyday Life: Moral Theology, Social Anthropology, and the Imagination of the Human*, Oxford: Oxford University Press, 2016.

Barth, Karl, *The Church Dogmatics IV/4: The Christian Life (Fragments)*, trans. Geoffrey Bromiley, Edinburgh: T&T Clark, 1981.

_____ *Ethics*, New York: Seabury Press, 1981.

_____ *The Holy Spirit and the Christian Life*, Louisville: Westminster John Knox, 1993.

Barton, Stephen C., *Life Together: Family, Sexuality and Community in the New Testament and Today*, Edinburgh: T&T Clark, 2001.

Basil the Great, *On Christian Doctrine and Practice*, New York: St Vladimir's Press, 2012.

_____ *On Christian Ethics*, New York: St Vladimir's Seminary Press, 2014.

Biggar, Nigel, *Aiming to Kill: The Ethics of Suicide and*

*Euthanasia*, London: Darton, Longman & Todd, 2004.

_____ *Behaving in Public: How to Do Christian Ethics*, Grand Rapids: Eerdmans, 2011.

Bonhoeffer, Dietrich, *Creation and Fall*, Dietrich Bonhoeffer Works, Vol. 3, Augsburg: Fortress, 2003.

_____ *Discipleship*, Dietrich Bonhoeffer Works, Vol. 4, Augsburg: Fortress, 2003.

_____ *Ethics*, Dietrich Bonhoeffer Works, Vol. 6, Augsburg: Fortress, 2005.

_____ *Life Together*, Bonhoeffer Works, Vol. 5, Augsburg: Fortress, 2005.

Bray, Gerald, *Creeds, Councils and Christ: Did the Early Christians Misrepresent Jesus?* Fearn: Mentor, 1997.

Bromiley, G. W., *The Unity and Disunity of the Church*, Grand Rapids: Eerdmans, 1958.

Chadwick, Henry, *The Early Church*, London: Penguin, 1993.

Chung, Paul, *The Spirit of God Transforming Life: The Reformation and Theology of the Holy Spirit*, New York: Palgrave Macmillan, 2009.

Clough, David, *On Animals, Vol. 1: Systematic Theology*, London: Bloomsbury, 2011.

_____ *On Animals, Vol. 2: Theological Ethics*, London: Bloomsbury, 2019.

Cranfield, C. E. B, *The Apostles' Creed: A Faith to Live By*, Edinburgh: T&T Clark, 1993.

_____ *A Critical and Exegetical Commentary on the Epistle to the Romans*, 2 vols, Edinburgh: T&T Clark, 1981.

Crisp, Oliver, 'On the Fittingness of the Virgin Birth', *Heythrop Journal* Vol. 99, 2008, 197–221.

Crossan, John Dominic, *Jesus: A Revolutionary Biography*, New York: Harper Collins, 1994.

Davis, Leo Donald, *The First Seven Ecumenical Councils (325–787): Their History and Theology*, Collegeville, MN: Michael Glazier/Liturgical Press, 1990.

Deane-Drummond, Celia and David Clough (eds.), *Creaturely Theology: On God, Humans and Other Animals*,

London: SCM Press, 2009.

Eilers, Kent and Kyle C. Strobel, *Sanctified by Grace: A Theology of the Christian Life*, London: T&T Clark, 2014.

Eusebius, *The History of the Church*, London: Penguin Books, 1989.

Fee, Gordon, *God's Empowering Presence: The Holy Spirit in the Letters of Paul*, Peabody, MA: Hendrickson Publishing, 1994.

George, Timothy, *Evangelicals and the Nicene Faith: Reclaiming the Apostolic Witness*, Grand Rapids: Baker Academic, 2011.

Gill, Robin (ed.), *The Cambridge Companion to Christian Ethics*, Cambridge: Cambridge University Press, 2001.

Gunton, Colin, *The Cambridge Companion to Christian Doctrine*, Cambridge: Cambridge University Press, 1997.

Gushee, David, *The Sacredness of Human Life: Why an Ancient Biblical Vision is Key to the World's Future*, Grand Rapids: Eerdmans, 2013.

Gustafson, James, *Christ and the Moral Life*, Chicago: University of Chicago Press, 1968.

Hall, Stuart, *Doctrine and Practice in the Early Church*, London: SPCK, 1994.

Hauerwas, Stanley, *The Work of Theology*, Grand Rapids: Eerdmans, 2015.

Holmes, Christopher R. J., *Ethics in the Presence of Christ*, London: T&T Clark, 2012.

_____ *The Holy Spirit*, New Studies in Dogmatics Series, Grand Rapids: Zondervan, 2015.

Holmes, Stephen and Murray Rae (eds.), *The Person of Christ*, London: T&T Clark, 2005.

Hovey, Craig, *Exploring Christian Ethics: An Introduction to Key Methods and Debates*, London: SPCK, 2018.

Humphrey, Edith, *Grand Entrance: Worship on Earth as it is in Heaven*, Grand Rapids: Brazos, 2011.

Jenson, Robert, *Canon and Creed*, Louisville: John Knox Press, 2010.

_____ *The Triune Identity: God According to the Gospel*, Augsburg: Fortress Press, 1982.

Kapic, Kelly (ed.), *Sanctification: Explorations in Theology and Practice*, Downers Grove, ILL:Inter-Varsity Press Academic, 2014.

Keck, Leander, *Who is Jesus? History in the Perfect Tense*, Edinburgh: T&T Clark, 2001.

Kelly, J. N. D., *Early Christian Creeds*, London: Longmans, Green & Co., 1950.

Kelly, Joseph, *The Ecumenical Councils of the Catholic Church: A History*, Collegeville, MN: Michael Glazier/Liturgical Press, 2009.

Kilner, John, *Dignity and Destiny: Humanity in the Image of God*, Grand Rapids: Eerdmans, 2015.

Kim, JinHyok, *The Spirit of God and the Christian Life: Reconstructing Karl Barth's Pneumatology*, Minneapolis: Fortress, 2014.

Lehman, Paul, *Ethics in a Christian Context*, Westport, CT: Greenwood Press, 1963.

Leyden, Michael, *Doctrine in Practice: Introducing Karl Barth's Moral Theology*, Cambridge: Grove, 2016.

_____ *Responsible Before God: Human Responsibility in Karl Barth's Moral Theology*, unpublished PhD thesis, University of Chester, 2014.

Lincoln, Andrew, *Born of a Virgin? Reconceiving Jesus in the Bible, Tradition, and Theology*, Grand Rapids: Eerdmans, 2013.

Loving, Robin, *Christian Faith and Public Choices: The Social Ethics of Barth, Brunner, and Bonhoeffer*, Philadelphia: Fortress Press, 1984.

Luckensmeyer, David, *The Eschatology of First Thessalonians*, Göttengen: Vandenhoeck and Ruprecht, 2009.

McFarland, Ian, *From Nothing: A Theology of Creation*, Louisville: Westminster John Knox, 2014.

Meilander, Gilbert and William Werpehowski (eds.), *The Oxford Handbook of Theological Ethics*, Oxford: Oxford University Press, 2007.

Messer, Neil, *Respecting Life: Theology and Bioethics*, London: SCM Press, 2011.

Moltmann, Jurgen, *Theology of Hope*, London: SCM Press, 1967.

Need, Stephen, *Truly Divine and Truly Human: The Story of Christ and the Seven Ecumenical Councils*, London: SPCK, 2009.

Nelson, R. David, Darren Sarisky and Justin Stratis (eds.), *Theological Theology: Essays in Honour of John Webster*, London: T&T Clark, 2015.

Norris, Richard, *The Christological Controversy*, Philadelphia: Fortress Press, 1980.

O'Donovan, Oliver, *Resurrection and Moral Order: An Outline for Evangelical Ethics*, Grand Rapids: Eerdmans, 1994.

Owens, L. Roger, *The Shape of Participation: A Theology of Church Practices*, Eugene, OR: Cascade, 2010.

Pelikan, Jaroslav, *Credo: Historical and Theological Guide to Creeds and Confessions of Faith in the Christian Tradition*, New Haven: Yale University Press, 2003.

_____ *Acts*, SCM Theological Commentary on the Bible Series, London: SCM Press, 2006.

Radner, Ephraim, *A Brutal Unity: The Spiritual Politics of the Christian Church*, Waco, TX: Baylor University Press, 2012.

Reinders, Hans, *Receiving the Gift of Friendship: Profound Disability, Theological Anthropology and Ethics*, Grand Rapids: Eerdmans, 2008.

Ritschl, Dietrich, *The Logic of Theology*, London: SCM Press, 1986.

Rutledge, Fleming, *The Crucifixion: Understanding the Death of Jesus Christ*, Grand Rapids: Eerdmans, 2015.

Salzman, Michele Renee, 'Christian Sermons against Pagans: The Evidence from Augustine's Sermons on the New Year and on the Sack of Rome in 410', in *The Cambridge Companion to Attila the Hun*, ed. Michael Maas, Cambridge: Cambridge University Press, 2014, 346–59.

Schmemann, Alexander, *Liturgy and Life: Christian*

*Development through Liturgical Experience*, New York: Orthodox Church in America, 1993.

Schweiker, William, *Responsibility and Christian Ethics*, Cambridge: Cambridge University Press, 1999.

Schultz, F. LeRon and Brent Waters (eds.), *Christology and Ethics*, Grand Rapids: Eerdmans, 2010.

Seitz, Christopher R. (ed.), *Nicene Christianity: The Future for a New Ecumenism*, Grand Rapids: Brazos, 2001.

Smith, James K. A., *Desiring the Kingdom: Worship, Worldview, and Cultural Formation*, Grand Rapids: Baker Academic, 2009.

_____ *You Are What You Love: The Spiritual Power of Habit*, Grand Rapids: Brazos, 2016.

Stevenson, J., *A New Eusebius: Documents Illustrative of the History of the Church to AD 337*, London: SPCK, 1980.

Stringfellow, William, *An Ethic for Christians and Other Aliens in a Strange Land*, Eugene, OR: Wipf and Stock, 2004.

Swinton, John, *Raging with Compassion: Pastoral Responses to the Problem of Evil*, Grand Rapids: Eerdmans, 2007.

Sykes, Stephen, *The Identity of Christianity*, London: SPCK, 1984.

Tanner, Kathryn, *Christ the Key*, Cambridge: Cambridge University Press, 2009.

Taylor, Charles, *The Ethics of Authenticity*, Cambridge, MA: Harvard University Press, 2003.

Taylor, Porter (ed.), *We Give Our Thanks Unto Thee: Essays in Memory of Fr. Alexander Schmemann*, Eugene, OR: Pickwick, 2019.

Thate, Michael, Kevin Vanhoozer and Constantine Campbell (eds), *'In Christ' in Paul: Explorations in Paul's Theology of Union and Participation*, Grand Rapids: Eerdmans, 2014.

Thielicke, Helmut, *Theological Ethics: Foundations*, Grand Rapids: Eerdmans, 1966.

_____ *Theological Ethics: Sex*, Grand Rapids: Eerdmans, 1979.

Thiselton, Anthony, *The Holy Spirit: In Biblical Teaching, through the Centuries, and Today*, London: SPCK, 2013.

Todt, Heinz Eduard, *Authentic Faith: Bonhoeffer's Theological Ethics in Context*, Grand Rapids: Eerdmans, 2007.

Torrance, Alan and Michael Banner (eds.), *The Doctrine of God and Theological Ethics*, London: T&T Clark, 2006.

Torrance, T. F., *The Trinitarian Faith*, Edinburgh: T&T Clark, 1988.

Travis, Stephen, *I Believe in the Second Coming of Jesus*, London: Hodder and Stoughton, 1983.

Van Buren, Paul, *The Austin Dogmatics 1957–58*, edited by Ellen Charry, Eugene, OR: Cascade, 2012.

Vanhoozer, Kevin, *Pictures in a Theological Exhibition: Scenes of the Church's Worship, Witness and Wisdom*, London: Inter-Varsity Press, 2016.

Verhey, Allen, *Reading the Bible in the Strange World of Medicine*, Grand Rapids: Eerdmans, 2003.

Vondey, Wolfgang (ed.), *The Holy Spirit and the Christian Life: Historical, Interdisciplinary, and Renewal Perspectives*, Basingstoke: Palgrave Macmillan, 2014.

Wainwright, Geoffrey, *Doxology: The Praise of God in Worship, Doctrine and Life*, London: Epworth, 1980.

Webster, John, *Confessing God: Essays in Christian Dogmatics II*, London: T&T Clark, 2005, 69–83.

_____ *The Domain of the Word: Scripture and Theological Reason*, London: T&T Clark, 2012.

_____ *God is Here! Believing in the Incarnation Today*, Basingstoke: Marshall Morgan & Scott, 1983.

_____ *Word and Church: Essays in Christian Dogmatics I*, Edinburgh: T&T Clark, 2001.

Wenham, David, *Paul: Follower of Jesus or Founder of Christianity?* Grand Rapids: Eerdmans, 1995.

Westcott, B.F, *The Gospel According to John*, London: John Murray, 1937.

Wiles, Maurice, *The Remaking of Christian Doctrine*, London: SCM Press, 1975.

_____ *Working Papers in Doctrine*, London: SCM Press, 1976.

Williams, Rowan, *Being Disciples: Essentials of the Christian Life*, London: SPCK, 2016.

_____ *Christ: The Heart of Creation*, London: Bloomsbury/Continuum, 2018.

_____ *Faith in the Public Square*, London: Bloomsbury, 2012.

Wolterstorff, Nicholas, *The God We Worship: An Exploration of Liturgical Theology*, Grand Rapids: Eerdmans, 2015.

Wright, D. F., (ed.), *Essays in Evangelical Social Ethics*, Exeter: Paternoster, 1978.

Young, Frances, *The Making of the Creeds*, London: SCM Press, 2002.

# Index of Biblical References

# INDEX OF BIBLICAL REFERENCES

*Titus*
1.7-9 168
2.12-14 137

*Hebrews*
2.10 120
4.15 103
5.1-5 103
5.8-9 120
11.3 57

*James*
2.18-24 12
5.7-8 137

*1 Peter*
1.11 149
2.9 17
2.11-17 85
2.18-25 120
2.13 84
3.22 84

*2 Peter*
3.12 137

*1 John*
2.1 151

*Revelation*
4.11 57, 59
17.14 81
19.16 81
21.1-4 56
22.20 76, 137

# Index of Names and Subjects